IN SEARCH OF KNOWLEDGE

IN SEARCH OF KNOWLEDGE

Jagdish Saran Sharma

GenNext Publication

Published by

GenNext Publication
5, Ansari Road
Daryaganj, New Delhi-110002
Phone: 011-47034999, 9811692060
E-mail: gennextpublication@hotmail.com

Distribution Network
gyanbooks.com
India, USA, Canada, UK, Australia, France

ISBN: 978-93-5663-101-4
"An Imprint of Kalpaz Publication"
First Published, 2023

Printed at: Gyan Press, Delhi.

IN SEARCH OF KNOWLEDGE

Author: Jagdish Saran Sharma

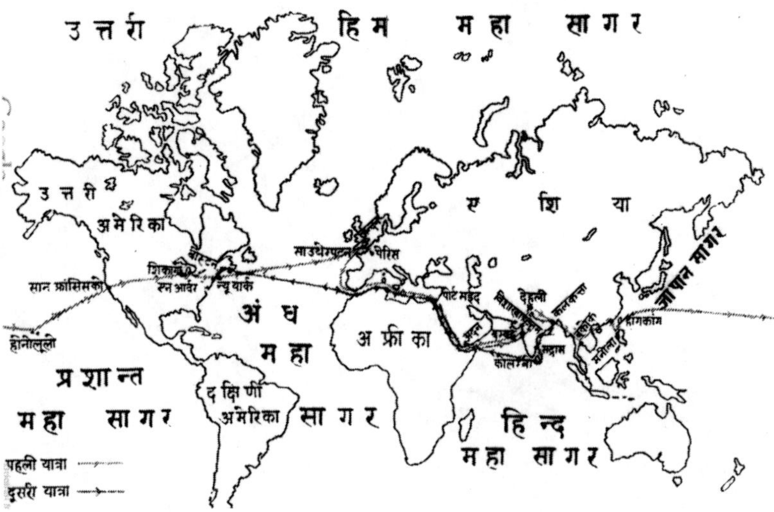

The Journey map of author – Novel translation into English – June 2022

In Search of Knowledge - ज्ञान-की-खोज-में

These letters were written during the period of 29 April 1953 (being the author's birthday) and 19 October 1954. The letters relate to his two journeys to USA. The first in order to complete his Master of Library Science starting August 1948 and returning August 1950 and the second to complete his PhD of Library science during the period July 1952 and October 1954.

All dates are nearly approximate.

Contents

Few words from the author

Since my childhood, I was fond of writing a daily diary in routine. When I got an opportunity to go overseas after completing my education at Delhi University, I experienced all the countries which came in way during the journey and penned all my experiences in diary. Fortunately, I received a Fellowship for PhD and went overseas for the second time. A thought struck in my mind to write a novel about the cultural, educational, financial, and social conditions of countries so that others also may get knowledge of these aspects during that era.

I got an opportunity to go overseas again soon after my marriage and I was willing to take my suave wife along: but she was about to become mother, so I could not take her. I sent my travel experiences to my wife in the form of letters so that she could know about my journey. I wrote all these letters in a very interesting and informative way and have compiled them as a novel here.

In this novel, I have not only discussed about the cultural and social believes of different countries and have expressed my views on the same. Also, I have covered my life and studies during my tenure overseas as demonstrated by reading this novel.

I am hopeful that our new generation would find it inspirational by reading this novel written during 1950s. Then only I would consider that my efforts are successful.

Finally, I would like to thank my wife and those friends who read these letters and encouraged me to compile my experiences in form of a novel. My special thanks to my friend and young Hindi writer and poet Mr. Kanhaiya Lal Chancharik who helped me in compiling and editing these letters into a novel.

I would like to thank the publisher Lala Shyamlal ji, owner of Bharti Sahitya Mandir for his efforts in publishing this novel.

— **Jagdish Saran Sharma**

(Translated from his original Hindi novel)

Prologue

Dedicated to our father and grandfather – Dr Jagdish Saran Sharma

Even though you passed away in January 1993 – you live amongst us through your academic work, family life and memories.

Gyan Ki Khoj Men (ज्ञान की खोज में) translates as "In Search of Knowledge". This travelogue novel was your first in Hindi and has recently been translated into English in June 2022. These are compilation of your letters to your wife (Prem Sharma - our mother and grandmother) whilst you travelled between India and Ann Arbour, Michigan USA for the purposes of your MA and subsequent PhD degrees in Library Science. The letters were written between 29 April 1953 and 19 October 1954 approximately.

As your children and grandchildren - we express our immense gratitude. The love, patience, care, and words of wisdom that you gave throughout your living years have been our guiding light. You are our inspiration to work harder, try more, and love fiercely. Because of your love, we are better human beings. Words can never express our appreciation – you have always been there for us. All we need in life is already in our hearts and our living memory of you.

As a family we are inseparable because we love each other unconditionally. This is something we learned from you. We also learned the value of hard work and ensuring one's family is always taken care of. Your love and compassion are embedded in our hearts and soul.

Thank you for always believing in us, even when we didn't believe in ourselves at times. You made us what we are today. You were an amazing father and grandfather - unfortunately you were taken too soon but your memories remain in our hearts and minds.

The translation and subsequent publishing of this book from Hindi is a testament to you and our tributes to you through the English translation for wider audience.

Sharma Family and Grandchildren
October 2022

1

My First Overseas Journey

927, Silven Avenue
N.R.Br,
Michigan (U.S.A.)
April 29, 1953

Dear Prem,

Today is my birthday, let it be. For me every day is important. Every moment just marks its presence in life and disappears somewhere. If I have started to write you the story of my first oversea journey during my second journey, then it is probably not for entertainment only. I wish you should not miss my presence while I am in a far land. I will try my best to write and send a bit of this long story once a week to you. I find two benefits by doing so. First, I will stay in practice to write Hindi. Secondly, when you read it in front of *Sabhyasanchi*, it will be good for him. He also won't miss my presence.

My first overseas journey started on 14 August 1948 at 6 AM when I boarded a Dakota of "Bharat Airways" for the first time in my life to reach Kolkata. It came to an end on 14 August 1950 when I landed at Mumbai from S.S. Kanton of P&O Lines, where my revered parents and well-wishers were waiting for me.

The thought of overseas travel and its glimpse

Babugarh Cantonment, which seems to be deserted today, used to be very happening place at a point of time. Flourishing farms used to be everywhere. Glittering and colourful bogies of British could be commonly seen running over the cemented roads. The charming flower beds on roadside. The dense branches of trees on both sides of road used to mingle in such a way as they were waiting someone to give-away a warm welcome. This whole environment could attract anyone to it. Babugarh used to be so happening that even thorn used to bloom. Who will not dive into joy by seeing such a mesmerizing beauty of nature.

I was not fortunate enough to witness the childhood and youth of Babugarh, but I have seen its old age, especially the last days very closely. When it was counting its last days disconcertedly. I have seen the last birds of this grove straying like nomadic clouds. Even today if I meet someone from those old days, they brace themselves and says "The world is quite fragile. Everything has an end".

I was born in a small village Ghazalpur located near Babugarh cantonment. There won't be more than 500 people in that village at that point of time. The piece of land which is the sole bread earner for them is surrounded by cantonment at one side and railways at another. The rear end is parted off by Kali River and provided to neighbouring village Dadayra, at the front side of it, which is mostly sandy, is shared with village Bigas, but still this village used to be happy and flourishing.

There is no school opened in Ghazalpur whilst these lines are being written. The students from this area are going to either cantonment or Hapur schools since ages and it continues. I was also enrolled in the old school of cantonment by my grandfather. I still remember that he distributed sweets among all the students. But I did not like to be there. Also, I used to cry a lot, and always felt like going home. Pandit Mathura Prasad was Headmaster those days. He was friend of my grandfather, used to adore me a lot and whenever I used to cry, he used to lure me by offering sweets. You will be surprised to know that while going to school with my friends in morning, I used to pray to God on daily basis that the school be closed but used to be upset finding the school opened.

But soon I started getting interested in school and studies were not a burden anymore. Daily morning moving out with friends with full-day meals in hand and returning back to home by evening, it became a routine for years. Babugarh cantonment was on our way to school, in fact our village was on one edge of it and the school was on another. Daily to and fro for two miles, it never felt tiring to walk four mile in a day. Grandmother use to keep hot milk ready as soon as I return from school. But sometimes she had to run behind me as I used to be busy playing.

There were many properties associated with cantonment, but which I feel most important was that the surrounding villages used to be very happy, and even today they are. The villages neighbouring to cantonment has better life than the ones use to be far from it. Even I was affected by it, whenever I used to see Bogies of British, cars and cycles, lot of questions used to arise in my mind. I used to be amazed by seeing tractors, harvesting machines, giant engines in fields. Sometimes I used to ask myself what is all this? Where did these machines come from? Why have they come? Who these British are? Why they are so fair? Which language do they speak? Why their clothes are better than us? Why they look stronger than us? Even their games used to amaze me sometimes. There was a Coffee House on our way, near to which they use to play cricket, tennis, Badminton and other games. I used to see them for long time, but passers-by were not allowed to stay there for a long time.

One fine day I tried to untwine my jumbled thoughts. I asked my grandmother where these British come and why? I remember, she said that they have come from Britain and they have acquired maximum land of our village. I understood from her words that villager did not like the arrival of the British. My grandfather was an influential personality. Everyone respected him. Any *Daroga (chief officer), Sepoy (Indian soldier serving under British), Tahsildar (Collector from Revenue Service) or Patwari (village revenue officer),* who used to come our village, used to visit him at the first place and my grandfather also used to welcome them whole-heartedly. I remember that once I have bitten on cheeks by a *Daroga*. I was very mischievous at that time, use to keep some or other issue ready for my grandfather.

It wasn't only the influence of cantonment which sow the seed of going abroad in my mind. Whenever I used to see the passing train making chug and chuffed, I used to think that where from this snake is coming and where it is heading to. My grandfather gave me lot of clarity on all this. My father who used to live in Delhi was willing to take me with him, but my grandmother didn't want as I was the only child at that time, and she wanted me to be with her. But my father brought me to Delhi in 1934 after 14 days of her death and enrolled me in Ramjas High School.

I passed my tenth grade in 1941. My father wanted me to become a doctor, but the almighty had other plans. I still didn't forget when my auntie's daughter Lakshmi was ill at Dr *Joshi's* hospital and her mother said that we don't have any doctor in our home. *Jagdish*, even you are not pursuing to be a doctor? In answer I said that I will be doctor for sure, but not of medicines. God kept my words, I passed B.A. (Hon.) in 1945. These four years were very significant. I could not study properly at home, so started to live at 'Boarding house'. The 'Boarding house' of Hindu college was very far from college. It is opposite to St. Stephen College. My room was adjacent to the road. The cross of St. Stephen College was visible from my window. Sometimes, the moon and its moonlight would peek in and talk to me through this window.

The seed of going abroad was already sown inside me from Babugarh cantonment. But I realized about it here only. I used to hear the speeches at St. Stephen College very attentively, I developed acquaintance with the professors there, a few of them were priest too. I got so interested that I enrolled myself in M.A. at St. Stephen College after completing B.A. (Hon.). Now the seed started sprouting and I completed my M.A. in 1947.

Before going to America, I had plans to go to London. I consulted my principal about it. He suggested me to stay at India for some more time and do some research. So, I enrolled myself to PhD at university and started research. But due to partition of India, my professor, who was my mentor too, moved to Pakistan. Now there was no professor left in university who was proficient with Mughal Era of Indian history. I was very puzzled, some of my friends were preparing for IAS. My principal asked me to attempt IAS exam but I had no interest. Many of my friends are IAS today and even I would have made it easily if tried. But I had some other dreams, it is about passion. I don't like the IAS life. There you have money and status, but don't have freedom as I wanted. Also, there were many restrictions.

I was very disappointed those days, how to take it forward! I was in my thoughts only, by the time a new department was opened in Delhi University. It was Library science. My plan was not only to become specialist of this subject rather to be expert of Archology and Archives. These subjects have very much importance in India today. See, what God's plan was.

2

Preparation for going abroad

927, Silven Avenue
N.R.Br,
Michigan (U.S.A.)
May 31, 1953

I have written to about my overseas journey and its background a month ago approximately. I was willing to write to you soon about the second chapter but could not do so, due to more work. Today it is Sunday, weather is also good. Flowers are blooming in front of my house, trees are swinging happily in fresh breezes of air. This attracts me towards it. I am staring at this continuously from my window. The moon is full of its charm and its light is coming to my room after getting filtered through the window. And I am writing to you: a story which has become a very important part of my life. I wish you knew about this part, that's why I am writing to you. Your memories are the core of my thoughts, the light if it's a lantern, its strength.

You would have heard the English phrase saying, "If wishes were horses, beggars might ride". It was very much with my preparations to go to America. It was a dream to go to America, and a passion to get higher education. But how it was possible for a common boy like me. The government in independent India has stopped scholarships. For the rich of the country, lending money for education was equivalent to committing a sin. There was a despair all around which wanted to shake my self-confidence completely.

I don't know how but I always find a ray of hope in despair. Despite of there being no reason, my heart was full of light, I was full of hope. Sailing through this hope and despair, I decided to continue my efforts! Let me do all the preparations which can be done without money, and let's see what happens ahead. So, I applied for a passport. I also applied to the four biggest universities of America. It was my luck that my passport got ready without any delay and on the other hand, the universities also accepted my application. Now the question was which university should I join? To get more clarity on this, I went to an officer, who was known to me and working at US embassy. By chance, the officer was a scholar of Michigan University. It was decided, I sent my consent letter to Michigan University and received my passport as well.

I find it important to write about how I managed the English clothes. As I said, I used to wear Kurta and *Pajama* made of *Khaddar (hand-spun and woven natural fibre cloth promoted by Mahatma Gandhi as swadeshi (self-sufficiency) for the freedom struggle of the Indian subcontinent).* Neither I was fortunate to get it washed at a laundry nor did I want to do so. I used to wash and iron my clothes myself. I had no idea about English clothes. But I had friends who used to wear coats and pants. I took advice from one of them. We decided to get suits stitched from Sharma tailors at Connaught place. I made two suits here and one at *Pandit* tailors. I learned how to wear a tie from him only. I told you in my earlier letter that I was pursuing "Library Science". Its exams were due in the last week of May. I was managing my studies with preparations. To bear my expenses, I had to take some tuition also. Life was busy and tough as always. My exams were over and results were declared by the end of June. I succeeded.

After the examination I invested all my time in preparations. I had to face challenges on every step. I know a few lucky students who need not to bother about anything but I am not one of them. I have only one thing by my side - believe in God. It feels thrilling to think about going to America but reality is not so. You need a lot of documents, letters and certificates. You cannot go there until you get Visa from the American government. You have to submit approximately eight documents to get it.

Somebody has said it right, when bad times come, it comes all over. I was in need of money. Also the doctor whom I went to the American embassy to get the certificate seemed to be a weird person. He troubled me a lot. It was not because my health was bad, but the doctors he wanted me to visit for blood tests, X-ray etc were expensive and I didn't want to go to them. But I had to go and he handed over the medical certificate to me. Got the medical certificate, now it was time for a bank statement. Only I know what all I had to face to get this. The memories of great help I received from my father will remain with me till my last breath. Such fathers are rare. Finally, I got my bank statement too.

I got the "Visa" from the American embassy after submitting all the necessary documents. I could enjoy this for a few moments only till I came to know from my "travel agent" that he could not arrange my passage. I felt disappointed. Thought to go to " India coffee house" and have a cup of coffee.

As soon as I entered, an old friend *Indra*, who was a student of D.Sc. in Delhi University those days called me. I went and sat beside him. Within no time he realized my mood and asked me for the reason. I told him the entire story. After the coffee he took me to a travel agent, where one of his friends was an assistant manager. A few moments after we arrived at the office, the Assistant manager received a telegram from a person stating that he cannot go to America due to health issues. My friend introduced me to him and talked about the reason for coming. For which he said that if I can deposit money in the next two hours and be ready to go to Calcutta by the next 6 AM flight, he will arrange passage for me. In that situation I didn't have a choice.

We were just coming out of the office when we found one of our friends outside with a car. Knowing the reason for my hurry, he said that he will take us to the bank. This help was sent by God! All three of us reached the bank and deposited money within one hour. I got my ticket. He gave me a small treat at the "Alps restaurant" situated on Queen's way.

Only 17 hours were left to leave Delhi. There was a lot to do and meet a lot of people. My friends dropped me at home. I informed my mother that I have to leave for America by 6:00 a.m. tomorrow. I went to my father's dispensary to inform him about it. Our family *Pandit Ji* came along with me to help me out for the preparations, meanwhile whoever my friends and well-wishers came to know about it they started to come home to meet me. It has continued till midnight. I had no sleep in my eyes and hardly slept for 2 hours that night. Got up at 4:00 a.m. in the morning, got ready and took a taxi before 5:00 a.m. and reached the airport. My uncle Sri Ramachandra and some well-wishers came along. At 6AM Bharat Airways' "Dakota" (plane) started its journey. It was the first air travel of my life.

3

Delhi to Calcutta

927, Silven Avenue
N.R.Br,
Michigan (U.S.A.)
June 07, 1953

As it is Sunday today l, slept till 7. Now it's 8 O'clock. After prayer and breakfast, now I have started to write to you about my first air travel from Delhi to Calcutta.

It must have been 4:55 in the morning when I started from home along with Sri Ramchandra ji and sister Lakshmi. It was dawn already. Date was August 14th. Weather was mild. Car was rapidly heading towards the airport. My mind was struggling with many thoughts. Emotions were swinging to and fro. Some unfamiliar happiness was visible on my face. When the taxi was crossing *Lal Quila* and *Chandni Chowk*, I suddenly looked towards my house and my eyes rested at Parade ground. The Silence of Pine trees at Edward Park was mesmerizing. I looked at *Faiz market* and Delhi Gate with greedy eyes and they were left behind within a few moments. The colourful market of Connaught Circus, which was staying in silence, disappeared. The delectable parts of Queensway, the trees and the bushes along the roadside, the bungalows, all were left behind and I felt that I am going away from all of them. Before 1 km to the airport my heart yearned with the imagination of losing Delhi. Within the next few moments, the taxi dropped me to the airport. I took my suitcase. Weighed myself and the suitcase and collected the ticket. The aircraft, which was supposed to take us along, was in front of me and few technicians were checking it.

Until this moment, I didn't realize that I am leaving behind my friends, relatives, city and motherland. Perhaps I was so busy in preparations that I did not get time to think about how much this separation would bother me. When there was only 10 minutes left to board the plane, I looked into the eyes of uncle *Ramchandra*. I offered garlands to my sister Lakshmi and Shravan, but when tears started to burst from everyone's eyes, I also lost my patience and my moist eyes also started to flow. For the next five minutes I forgot everything and started thinking, "What is all this? Why am I going?" And many more questions arose. Then my mind went into the history. When ancient explorers used to go abroad. It is a far better situation today as there are better facilities available. I consoled myself.

There were only 5 minutes left for 6 AM. The aircraft door opened and passengers were asked to board. I touched my father's feet, hugged uncle *Ramchandra*, sister Lakshmi etc. and moved towards the door. I was feeling a little suffocated, tears were flowing continuously. The aircraft started to float in the air, and I was still looking towards them with teary eyes from the window. It was the same feeling when I was looking at you on 20 July 1952 when you disappeared from my eyes with the departure of "S.S. City of Cape town".

As I already mentioned, it was my first overseas trip. As soon as we entered the plane, we were told to fasten the seat belt and cotton was provided to plug into the ears. I plugged the cotton and kept looking down the window. As we kept going higher, things turned to be tinier, Yamuna was looking like a twisted thread and trees were looking just like a green spot.

After some time, a cup of coffee and some biscuits were served in a beautiful tray. Due to feeling upset and weeping I had a mild headache. Coffee did its job and I felt refreshed. After finishing my coffee, I started looking down and continued till Nagpur.

We would have stayed for 20 minutes at Nagpur, three passengers left while 5 boarded the plane. Three of them seemed to be businessmen while one lady was with her daughter, maybe 5 years old. From Delhi there were maybe 8 people, most of them looked like businessmen. There was one leader from Bengal who was also a member of the constituent assembly. This gentleman was wearing Khaddar clothes and so was I. Suddenly he asked me where I was going and I told everything. I think he already got an idea as he was staring at me for quite some time. He gave me a serious look and asked if I had any arrangements for my stay at Calcutta? I said that I will stay with my friend. This gentleman seemed to be a humble person. Aged around 60 years. All others in the plane were lost in their own world, neither had they had spoken to me nor I did.

I had heard that "air sickness" troubles the passengers a lot. That's why paper bags are kept near passengers so that they can use it if they feel like vomiting. I did not feel "air sickness" till Nagpur. But after leaving Nagpur, the girl sitting next to me started vomiting so I also started feeling alike. I tried to control it for some time. But when suddenly the plane took a dive and suddenly started to regain the height, I lost my control. I picked a paper bag and tried to vomit but could not. But my stomach was not alright.

When we reached near Calcutta, the speed of the plane was decreased slightly. I was looking down continuously. Greenery was spread all over. Coconut trees were standing with pride. Houses with the red tile roof were adding a strange beauty to the scenery, looking like a pulpy green mango has started to ripe. All passengers started to exit after the plane landed.

It would be around 2 o'clock. Sky was clear, the sun was mild, but the air was not like Delhi, it was a little moist. My suitcase was loaded on a big truck and the passengers were informed that the bus of "Bharat Airways" will leave for the city office in 20 minutes. I had given prior information to my friend about arriving at Calcutta. I informed him by telephone after reaching the airport. He promised to meet me at the city office 20 minutes passed quickly. The passengers who did not have any other arrangements of transportation, sat in the bus and the bus started. It was my first time in Calcutta. I felt something new seeing the crowd here. Every moment was a new experience. Within no time we started to move across the big market and finally the bus reached the "Bharat Airways" office.

I was just getting off the bus when I heard the classical tone of my friend "*Jagdish*, you have come". We came home by taxi, my friend introduced me to his parents, wife, and kids. After some time I took a bath and changed my clothes. It was August 14th. Places were being decorated with lights, flags and festoons. My friend took me to visit *Chaurangi Maidaan* and Victoria memorial. You must be remembering how we both sat at a bench near Victoria memorial on 19 July 1952, the same way we both friends sat there for long. Around 11 o'clock we returned home and I went into a deep sleep.

Next day when I woke up the sun was already up. I finished breakfast after taking a bath and prepared a schedule for the full day. I had a lot of important work to accomplish. Had to collect travel cheques from "American Express" and get a travel ticket in turn of American Airways voucher. Also had to ensure the flight details and date of travel. My friend and I went to the market and checked if the travel agent's office was closed on the occasion of 15th August. It was closed. I had to change all my schedule. Then we went to my friend's office where he was a manager.

We came home for lunch after spending 3 hours at the office. Took some rest after lunch and again left for the market. I had to buy some necessary things which I could not buy in Delhi due to hurry. One of our Bengali friends invited us to a function in the evening. We had dinner in a Chinese restaurant after this. Then we enjoyed the lights at Chaurangi Maidan and Victoria memorial and came back home. Those days my friend was writing a novel. He read me a chapter of it which was very interesting. Now it is published with the title "*Ekaki*". We slept after some time.

On August 16th morning, I went to the "travel agent" office. It was very crowded. This year approximately 200 students were going to America. The Indian government had booked an "American Airways" plane for us and we had to reach Hong Kong by this in batches. From Hong Kong we had to board the ship S.S. Meags of "American President Lines". My turn was on August 17th and I departed at 1 AM with 60 other students.

4

Calcutta to Siam

927, Silven Avenue
N.R.Br,
Michigan (U.S.A.)
June 21, 1953

Today is Sunday. It's 9 o'clock in the morning. I have just finished breakfast. As you know I keep breakfast simple. Two apples, two bananas and a cup of coffee. Now I will have dinner directly as I only have food once on Sundays. It keeps my body healthy and sane. I have already said that I always try to keep my thoughts in control. So far, this has been very simple and disciplined. Despite living in a country like America, I am untouched by its materialism. Whatever I like in this place, I adopt it in my life, whatever does not coincide with my principles, I don't pay attention to it. Life is going on like this only.

Obviously whatever thing or thought I feel is correct, I try my best to maintain it. Pursuing higher education is best among all of them, this is my belief.

I wrote to you upon reaching Dumdum airport on June 7th. To reach the airport, we all had to assemble at the "Grand Hotel". From there Pan American Airways buses took us to the airport. My friend dropped me off at "Grand Hotel" by 11 o'clock. We had to be there by 12 o'clock. Now the question was how to spend one hour. I wrote earlier also that these days every moment of my life is very important. There were all new faces around in the waiting room. The total count of people boarding 1 AM flight today was about 50. It seems like they were from almost every part of India.

My mind was swinging between happy and sad thoughts. Remember home and country on one side and feeling happy to go overseas for higher studies on the other. Time was passing rapidly. It was not affected by any emotion. Got introduced to a few passengers sitting there. From where they are coming and which American university they are going. One hour passed just like that. We were informed that buses are ready and we can board with our luggage to reach the airport. I picked my suitcase and started moving. Our luggage was loaded onto a truck and we sat into the bus to reach the airport. After about 5 minutes, the bus started to move across the silent roads of Calcutta. It was 12 o'clock already but still cars could be seen commuting on the road. A pleasant wind was blowing. As far as the bus was moving, the colourful Calcutta was leaving behind. When our bus reached the open area after crossing all the big markets, the wind happened to be more pleasant. My mind was experiencing very strange emotions.

When we were about one mile away from the airport, we saw the plane landing. It drew all my attention towards the airport and I came out of my thoughts. Our bus reached the airport lounge and people started getting down. Also our luggage was being unloaded from the truck. All of us collected our luggage and got it weighed. A sticker with the owner's details was pasted on every small and big suitcase and it was sent to the plane before us. Calcutta police verified and stamped our passport and other necessary documents. The doctor from Airways verified our certificates for Cholera, Chicken Pox and Yellow Fever and we were told to go inside. Our plane was ready. We were told to sit inside; I remembered God and took a seat.

This plane was 6 times bigger than the plane on which I was traveling from Delhi to Calcutta. I remember it had 6 engines. Approx. 60 or 65 passengers were there. Even its height was ample at the centre, anyone could stand comfortably without leaning. Seats were also very comfortable with sufficient leg space. A blanket and pillow was given to every passenger. It was my second chance on a plane; hence it did not feel anything new. The turbulence was minimal on this plane and was very much comfortable. I did not feel air sickness at all till Bangkok. We were offered snacks after some time. I took two bananas and a cup of coffee and started to talk to the passenger sitting next to me. He was a *Madrasi* gentleman. Son of some big government officer. He looked to be very royal but humble at the same time. It happened to be 2 o'clock while we were talking. Then this gentleman slept. I also started trying to sleep; but I don't sleep during travel. Still I closed my eyes. I slept for some time. I had to wake up suddenly after one hour. There was turbulence in the air, there was a small sandstorm. It brought trouble for the pilot. But the sandstorm reduced around 6 o'clock and the sunrise also came up.

When the plane landed in Bangkok, it was 7 o'clock in morning. We had to halt here for approximately 1 hour as passengers had to take breakfast and the plane had to be refilled with fuel. We all came down one by one. Pleasant air was breezy. It was green all around. The big leaves of banana trees looked like the ears of an elephant. Seemed like they were dancing with the breeze of air too. The airport building was mostly made of wood. Roofs were mostly tiled. They were all covered with flower vines which looked pretty.

We were informed about the washroom. I went and took a bath. Then I entered a big room. It was a nice room; our plane could be seen from here. It had three big tables covered with white table covers. Fruits, knife-fork and napkins etc. were kept over them. All passengers sat for breakfast. A waiter came to me with eggs. I smiled at him and told him that for me oats, milk, toast, fruits and tea will be sufficient. I had a heavy breakfast. The fruits here were very delicious, especially bananas and *chakotara Pomelo – Grapefruit)*. This was a too luxurious breakfast for a person like me, but I had to be luxurious when offered.

We were about to finish breakfast when we got an announcement that the flight will be delayed by 3 hours due to bad weather. I discussed this with some of my friends to utilize this time. I had already confirmed with a map that Bangkok city was not far from this place, hence why we shouldn't use the opportunity to see the new city. Few of them liked my suggestion and we enquired about it. I went to the office with two friends to see if any taxi or bus was available. Luckily there was a bus available. But we had to get permission to visit Bangkok. I had already incorporated an endorsement from the Thailand embassy and paid fees for it as suggested by my travel agent at Delhi, so I didn't have any issue, but my friends had to take permission. We sat in the bus and travelled to Bangkok immediately once permission was granted.

Bangkok, whose population is 688,832 is the capital of Thailand or Siam. It is situated at the bank of Menem River near Bay of Siam and is the commercial centre of Siam. Rice, tin, teak, and rubber are exported from here. Rice cleaning and boat making workshops can be commonly seen here. It is connected to Singapore, Chiang Mai and Prompinnh by railway.

Bangkok seems to be an ancient city. Houses and temples with Buddhist architecture can be seen here. In the 19th century, houses started to be constructed in European style here. Since then, Christian missionaries started to visit here in big numbers. Grand palace and Dusit palace are the prominent buildings here. Due to lack of time, we could not see these places from inside, but we took a glance at some places in the city. We returned back to the airport in an hour and half. Came to know that the plane is ready to leave in half an hour. At 11 o'clock we boarded the plane again and it took off.

5

Siam to Hong Kong

927, Silven Avenue
N.R.Br,
Michigan (U.S.A.)
August 01, 1953

I am writing to you again after 5 weeks as I am in the mood of writing today. Hong Kong was interesting as it was smaller than Bangkok. It was more interesting to see down through the window as the view was entirely different. We were flying above the sea and hence it was blue everywhere. Sometimes one or two mountains also happened to be seen. Speed of air was quite low but after a flight of two hours, dark clouds began to form in the sky and air turbulence started, it created trouble for the pilots. Hence they took the plane to the altitude higher to the clouds. Sometimes the plane was above the clouds and sometimes it was dropping below them. These shifts were felt in my stomach.

You may ask how passengers come to know about the altitude of the plane. It's a rule to inform passengers about the altitude, location and destination of the plane every hour through a chart. All of us were very tense due to the turbulence, few started to vomit while others were scared. This continued for two hours.

After flying for five hours, we started to see the range of dark mountains. Rain also stopped, speed of wind had also reduced and planes were flying normally now. It was time for breakfast. But I was willing to go to the lavatory once as I took a diet of fruits and milk that day. You must be thinking about how a plane lavatory would be. It used to be at the end of the plane with all necessary arrangements. A person can easily stand but cautiously, railings are placed there to hold if required. After coming out of the lavatory, I just fell to my seat. Immediately a cup of coffee, apples, grapes etc. were served. I was not in a mood to spare anything. I ate everything and had coffee at last, it felt really healing. After breakfast I started feeling sleepy, hence I slept for half an hour.

The *Madrasi* gentleman sitting next to me got so amazed that he woke me up and said, "See what a beautiful view!" At first, I didn't feel good about it but later when I saw the view, I realized what I could have missed.

Our plane was flying above Hong Kong airport and was about to land. The view below was so fascinating and beautiful that I cannot forget it in my entire life. On one side mountains and tidy roads and beautiful houses built over them, while the deep blue sea on another side. Sun rays were glittering in the water and spreading a strange aura. Our plane was in the lap of such a beauty of nature. Hong Kong port is a small but such a beautiful port. Mountains at three sides and the deep blue sea at fourth, looks like a pan to cook vegetables. After getting down from the plane, our passports were verified and luggage was screened. Once we were done with this and came out of the custom house, an old Chinese person was distributing two glass bottles along with his young partner. I felt weird about such a welcome, hence I asked the old man why he is distributing the bottles. Old man replied in a clear voice that tomorrow all of us have to undergo a medical examination and we have to be there with urine and stool samples. I felt like laughing and felt sad as well at the same time. One week back only, we had undergone all this. Anyhow, the next day we visited the doctor and paid the fees of Rupees 35. In my opinion, it was unnecessary.

Since there were no rooms available in hotels, the stay arrangements for our entire batch were done at a Christian missionary high school situated upon a hill. It was really a nice place. Calm and nicely arranged. There were 25 passengers in every room. Actually it was a boy's dormitory. We were charged for a decent hotel. In reality, we were looted, but we had to deal with it as we did not have any other option.

The evening when we reached Hong Kong, we had our dinner and slept after gossiping for some time. Next day we woke up, took breakfast after bath and reached a big hotel for medical examination where other Indians were staying. After that I went sightseeing with a few friends.

Hong Kong is an island. It is a small place and under the control of the British. It is divided into two parts. Sea happened to be in between. We have to take a boat to travel from one part to another. It was my first time to sit in such a big boat. We went to the city by boat and visited shops. Some of my friends went shopping. It seemed like goods were cheaper at this place. I purchased a few photographs and postcards and sent them to my friends. Whole day was spent roaming and we returned, had dinner and slept.

Next day a student from school came to us and started talking to us. He seemed to be a student of class tenth and a nice boy. He told us that he is the son of a big officer. He invited us to his home and said that he will show us the nicest things of Hong Kong. I looked at my friends in order to respond to his offer and we accepted his invitation. Four of us started, took the boat, and reached another shore in 15 minutes.

Our new Chinese friend was our guide now. He was showing us new things by pointing to them. There are plenty of Indians too. Soldiers are mostly Sikh, while traders are Sindhi and Marwari. Sometimes he took us to his home which was in a nice society. His home was a nice two-story bungalow decorated in British style. There was no one at home at that time except two servants. Four of us had lunch and moved on for roaming. The Chinese boy was still with us. He dropped us back to school and then went back to his home. We took a bath, had dinner, gossiped for some time, and then slept.

On the fourth day, our Chinese friend had promised to take us to the hill by electric train. At 9 o'clock, he reached school. Four of us started to climb the hill. All of us purchased our own tickets after reaching the station and sat into the train. When I looked down, the view was beautiful but scary as the train was going very fast. Finally we reached the peak. There was a small hotel near the station. Our friend offered us tea, we had tea and moved on. This place was considered a nice tourist spot as *Chaupati* Beach in Bombay and India Gate in Delhi. But there were a lot of photographers as you would have seen at *Jama Masjid* and *Lal Quila*. These photographers started asking us for photographs. We consulted and decided to get one picture and everyone has to pay equally. I still have one copy of it in my collection, I will show you someday.

As I already wrote, the British constructed big houses and roads on these hills. They were all covered with streetlights. When its reflection used to appear in the sea at night, it happened to be very amazing. I have a "Picture postcard" of this view in my collection.

Fifth day we stayed at school. Day passed well. We were busy packing the luggage and handing it over for loading in the evening. At 12 o'clock in night, we boarded the ship whose name was S.S General Meags. It was a troopship of American airlines which was converted to passenger ship. It was huge, had approx. 5000 passengers, mostly Chinese.

A market in Hong Kong city

6

Hong Kong to San Francisco

It was around 11 o'clock in night. We all reached the ship S.S General Meags after loading our luggage. There was a hill opposite to the ship and houses were constructed over it. The reflection of lights from these houses on the sea were looking beautiful. Our ship was also glittering. Initially it was a warship but later converted to passenger ship. It had fought and won a battle against Japan in the Pacific Ocean. It weighed more than 25 thousand tonnes and it was among the fastest ships. Its average speed was 21 miles per hour which was known to be very fast. At wartime, it could carry 10,000 soldiers but only 5,000 passengers could be accommodated.

Approximately 3,000 Chinese nationals boarded from Hong Kong, most of which were going to America. Rest were Japanese, British, American, Hawaiian and Indian. We were 200 approx. Most of us were students. This ship had two classes - like any other ship. First class was in the top two decks. Rest of the area had an engine store and our royal class. Since our class had more people, it was spread over five floors. Unfortunately, we got seats on the lowest floor, under the water level. Ventilators were not natural; the air was blowing with machines. It used to be a bit discomfort during the malfunctioning of ventilators. There was no washroom or lavatory available on this floor and we had to go to the upper floor for it. There was an electric fountain on this floor which used to provide drinkable water by pressing the button. But sometimes it used to not work. After all, it is a machine.

This entire floor was allocated to Indians. There were some essentials kept on one side, but there was interference due to it. We were provided bunk beds where we had to jump to reach the upper bed. I chose the upper bed considering it will be cleaner and separated.

I had entered the ship very eagerly. Had a small bag in hand which had the necessary documents and passport. Also one coolie was along with luggage. He took me four floors down and left. There were some more friends too. But some weird smell over there ruined all my eagerness to go to America. It was not a bad smell for ship staff, for them it was just a pesticide. But since I never smelt it before and it was sprayed in excess, it was a big discomfort for me. But I had to be there, what could've been done. I just arranged my bed and luggage, covered my nose with a handkerchief and ran out of there.

There was no deck available in our class, there was not an appropriate open space too. Normally it used to be in all passenger ships but it was not a passenger ship. I used to feel uncomfortable going down, then I decided to not to go down until and unless it was really necessary. I didn't have a blanket or extra suit. Carrying the blanket provided down the floor was not allowed. Sleeping at night was a big challenge. Luckily, I happened to meet *Chaudhary Jaat the next* day. He was from the neighbourhood of my mother's village and he knew my grandparents and uncles. While we were talking to each other, matter of foul smell came into discussion. He said that he was also troubled with this and he already brought a blanket up and is going to sleep here only at night. He had one military blanket and an old overcoat. He told me to sit along and I could use them as well. I was very relaxed with this. We started to stay together mostly since that day. This person was a vegetarian too and used to hate meat. That's why both of us use to manage with fruits, tea, coffee, potatoes, roti etc. There was no proper place to sit on the deck, so we used to kill time by sitting over some machine or likely place. When it used to rain at night, I used to hide under the shade of some machine. Actually, I realized the crux of Bhajan *'Raghu Pati Raghav Raja Ram' (pious Indian prayer)* here only. When sitting lonely at night, I used to recite it, used to feel calm then and night happened to pass. This was how I managed the nights.

Food was another issue on this ship. Since most of the people were in this second class, there was not sufficient space for all of them to take food at once. It used to be in two batches and we had to be in queues to take food. It was my first experience to have food while standing. It was very uncomfortable in the beginning but I managed later. I used to take vegetables only. Used to take milk, sugar, coffee as well.

Three to four days were passed like this only. On fifth day, I spoke to my vegetarian colleagues. I said if we go and meet captain and ask him that we would like to cook Indian vegetarian food ourselves. They liked my suggestion. But I had never spoken to a captain and hence we needed an experienced person. Luckily one student among us had already been to America earlier and was going again to try his luck at Hollywood cinema. He agreed and we five representatives went to the captain. He denied initially but later agreed with a condition to deposit 1 dollar as extra labour fees. We agreed to his condition and then vegetables were cooked in Indian style. It was much relaxing to the stomach. He was the same gentleman who travelled Mathura to Delhi with us if you remember. I even introduced him with you. His name is Mr. Bhatia.

Our ship was welcomed with a heavy storm in the China Sea. Our ship was as helpless as any other small boat in front of waves. Its speed was reduced and sometimes the tides used to rise up to the fifth floor. The tumbler kept over the table used to fall, even walking inside the ship was difficult. Vomiting people could be seen everywhere. Almost everyone was affected by sea sickness. Even I was not well. At first I was not comfortable with the food, but now I was not even able to drink milk. Only I could eat some oranges. It continued for 48 hours. The sea was calm and steady after crossing the Chinese sea but the speed of the ship remained slow.

The Pacific Ocean has many beautiful islands. They are called Hawaii islands and Manila is their capital. Our ship reached Manila port after one week. Only a few people left the ship. Fewer of them were Indians too who were coming directly from Calcutta. Our ship was there for 8 hours. I sent some letters to India and we Indians went down after permission from immigration officer. Rented a bus to see Manila city. It's a very beautiful city. Mountains all around covered with green trees.

Maybe you would like to know more about Manila, so I am writing about it. Manila is the capital and largest port of the Philippine republic. Its population is 143,906 as per the 1949 census. These islands were under the control of Spain till 1762 when the British captured it. The British control did not last long as Spain reclaimed it after 2 years. But it was captured by America after the Spanish American war and till date it is controlled by America. During World War 2, a big war was fought here and it went into Japanese control during 1842 -1945. After the defeat of the Japanese, America reclaimed it and now it is a republic like India. Here are universities too and one of them is Philippine university. My friend Mr. *Saxena* was a teacher here for 2 years. All the library expenses of this university are borne by our Michigan University.

I drank Coca-Cola for the first time at Manila port. One Philippine orchestra also boarded the ship from here which gave us the opportunity to listen to Philippine music three times during our journey. Evening about 6 o'clock our ship started from here. We were on the way to Honolulu port now.

You must be finding this name very strange. Even I found it strange when I heard it for the first time. We arrived here after one week. Maybe you would like to know about this city, so I am writing in brief summary. Honolulu is the capital of Hawaii. Its population is 257,696. It is a prominent port of Hawaii. It's a very beautiful place. Americans come here for vacation. It is a producer of sugarcane, pineapple, coffee and other fruits. City is small but there is plenty of sea. We could not get down here as dock staff was on strike. Ship also could not stay here for more than 2 hours.

When it was only two day's left for our voyage, we Indians had a meeting. Songs were sung in regional languages, and other games were also played. But one strange thing happened too. Some people were willing to pass a motion against the bad arrangements made by the Indian government and send it to the education ministry. It was agreed in unison but opinion differed on the usage of words. This went up to the extreme and turned into abuse and somehow manhandling did not happen. There was more dispute between *Biharis* and *Bengalis*. It was not their fault though; its foundation was laid by the British. The sad thing which could be seen in today's India is casteism, provinciality and discrimination. Top of that we all had different languages. If there was a common language, it was English, the imposed one, the symbol of slavery. Finally, the idea of motion was dropped.

In today's journey, there were few unforgettable moments too. The sunrise and sunset used to look magnificent from the sailing ship. When the sun sets, its reflection spreads all over the sea which is a treat to watch. Same is for the full moon night also.

The moonlight resembles a blooming bell flower. Looks like a sheet of silver is spread and waving as far as you can see. It was the first time when I realized what beauties are hidden in the treasure of nature. At this time, I used to remember the Almighty and used to think how beautiful he would be who has created all this.

We had many Sardarji with us and one of them was very interesting. He used to call himself *Kashmiri*. Age might be 20 years. Lean body and humble nature. He was very fond of reading hands. When we came to know about it, few people started visiting him just for fun while some went seriously and started to ask him about their destiny. He also used to say something jovial and what they wanted to hear. It continued for 3-4 days; but once this news got more viral, *Sardarji u*sed to be surrounded by crowds all the time. Most of them were girls. He used to tell fate the way it used to fit the situation and used to joke a lot.

There were many jovial people too in this Indian group. By chance we felt hungry one midnight. One *Khan Sahib* was also there among these hungry people. He was from Lucknow; another was one *Sharma ji* who was from either Allahabad or Lucknow. Their beds were also adjacent in the lower row. There was a *Madrasi* gentleman in the upper row, aged approx. 45, he had many boxes with him consisting of chilli powder, spices and almonds. *Madrasis* are fond of chilli and spices very much and add them additionally to the food. *Khan Sahib* had seen him buying almonds one day but was not sure in which box almonds were kept. He slowly climbed up and started checking all the boxes. His hand hit the box of chilli powder and the chilli powder was scattered. Some of it scattered on people sitting down. Some of the *Madrasis* woke up during all this happening. Nothing happened for two minutes as everyone was amazed and silent, in which Khan Sahib kept walking with the almond box. After a while the chillies started to affect people, all they stood up and we enjoyed the situation. This happened two days before reaching San Francisco.

I had seen one more prominent thing. Few people on the ship started to think that it would be impossible to survive here without consuming meat, alcohol and cigarettes. Many friends who were not into it started to consume meat and alcohol. I read about the same situation in the biography of *Subhash babu* (Subhash Chandra Bose) and committed myself that I will never consume meat, alcohol or cigarettes in any condition. I am happy that God has helped me to keep my words and till date I have never touched these and it did not lead to any physical or mental loss to me. I would also like to write here that there are many misconceptions about the West but they are not true. A person can live here the way he wants, it totally depends upon him.

Our voyage was about to end. I slept downstairs only that night. Reason was I had to pack my bags and also it had started to get cold. Apart from this I had to meet all the friends and note their addresses. That night we did not even sleep completely. We were gossiping till 2 O'clock. Then I went to my bed and slept. About 5 AM, I woke up when a friend came shouting that the Golden Bridge of San Francisco was visible. Me and many others quickly wore the clothes and rushed up. There was fog and lightning everywhere. We enquired and understood that the dock was still too far.

We came back downstairs and started preparations. I got fresh, took a shave and went for a bath and was about to change my clothes.

Around 7 o'clock, almost all the passengers were in their suits. Most of them were wearing hats too. Some started to smoke cigars, cigarettes and pipes. I started thinking after seeing all this. Decided that I will get down in *Sherwani* and *Khaddar* clothes. I was very happy to see that three more people were in the same attire.

It would be 10 o'clock in morning when our ship reached San Francisco port. Education minister and his assistant from the Indian embassy came to welcome us by small boat. They met us and shared necessary information. I knew one of them. He was the brother of Mrs. *Aruna Asif Ali.*

Since there were more passengers and everyone had to undergo a medical examination, it went up to 6 o'clock in the evening. Medical certificates and other documents for each and every passenger were verified which we had collected from the American embassy. After verifying all the documents thoroughly, immigration officer allowed all of us to leave the ship.

After getting free of customs, me and some of my friends decided about the hotel. Some people went to expensive hotels as their expenses were borne by the Indian government. But whoever did not want to spend much, came to Goldfield Hotel with us. The owners of this hotel were *Gujarati.* Hotel was small but homely. Food was also Indian.

7

San Francisco to Ann Arbour

927, Sylvan Avenue
N.R.Br,
Michigan (U.S.A.)
September 29, 1953

I got free from immigration officers and customs by 4 o'clock in the evening. The sun was in its full shine and it seemed like it would be late for evening. My assumption was correct, I came to know that sun sets here by quarter to eight. The friends who had decided to stay at Goldfield Hotel, came out of the custom office with their luggage, where a queue of taxis stood. There were many types of taxis but there were many called yellow cabs. Mr. Bhatia, who was our companion or rather he was our leader. He talked to the taxi drivers, and we sat in the taxis and came in front of the Goldfield Hotel. When I came out of the customs office and stood on the side of the road, I felt for the first time that I was standing in a new country. The roads were wide and clean. Cars were running very fast. Instead of the traffic police at the intersections of the roads, there were red, yellow, and green traffic lights, as you might have seen in Calcutta. There were big, decorated shops in the markets. The display windows, which were found in all the shops here, were richly decorated. In the display windows of clothing stores stood mannequin of men and women dressed in a variety of suits. Also saw many fruit shops in which the fruits were neatly arranged. Oranges, grapes, pineapple and apples were to be seen in abundance. All this seemed like a dream to me. Standing up, it seemed as if I was still on the ship.

Our taxi stopped in front of Goldfield Hotel. The driver opened the door and I got down with my three other companions. The taxi driver saw the meter and told the fare. Mr. Bhatia paid the money. Along with this, a tip was also given to the driver. Here the tip means 10% has to be given.

If the taxi fare is $1, a 10 cent tip should be given. Taking our belongings, we entered the lobby of the hotel and we were welcomed by two Indians. One of them will be around 55 years old and the other was around 30 years old. The owners of this hotel were elderly men, who came here about 30 years ago and were Gujarati brothers. After a while we were taken to our respective rooms. In this hotel, as in all hotels, there were two types of rooms, one single and the other double. I and my colleague named *Sachchidanand* Sharma were staying in the same room. This gentleman had come from Bombay and was fluent in Gujarati. He could also speak Marathi well. He was very jolly and cheerful.

When we came to our room, we took some rest. After washing hands and face, which was arranged in the room itself, we made a program to go to the market. Actually I just wanted to rest. But this companion of mine did not bring any English suits from India. He had to get a suit, so I had to go with him. We were both wearing *Sherwani* and *Churidar pyjamas*. We left the hotel and headed towards the clothing stores. Perhaps you do not know that almost all the shops here are of readymade suits. Suits prepared by measurement are very expensive here and only few choose to get them made, otherwise thousands of suits are made in hundreds of sizes. Here the suit shops are very big and the suit which you select after trial can be purchased immediately. In the same way, suits for ladies are also available. You will also be interested to know that the shops here are open only from 10 am to 5 pm. Sunday is a holiday and Saturday is open from 10 am to 1 pm. Some shops are open for more than a few hours on a particular occasion i.e. on days when sales are high. Otherwise, these shops keep fixed opening and closing timings. Here, for an hour of modest work, you get about five rupees to ten rupees. Some even get two rupees; somebody even gets ten rupees. Those whose job is permanent and better; they get at least twenty rupees per hour. Here any man or woman can live well by working 5 hours a day. Jobs are easily available. Unemployment definitely persists here too, but it is very less. We walked around the market for about 1.5 hours and then came back to the hotel. We also ate the food in the hotel itself which was Indian. After having dinner, we came to the drawing room of the hotel. Gossiped for some time, some more Indians also came who had lived in San Francisco for a long time. One of them was even from the time of *Lala Lajpat Rai*. He asked many things about India, also asked where we have come from, what are the subjects and where are we going here. While gossiping it was 12 o'clock. Then we went to our respective rooms and slept.

My eyes opened the next day at seven. There was silence everywhere in the hotel, everyone seemed to have slept late. Everyone was still asleep. I silently got up and went to the washroom, shaved and washed my face. By 8 o'clock everything was done. My companions had also got up and were ready to go to the washroom. I had decided to wear an English suit on this day. I had brought only two suits with me. One of them was a "Gabardine" worth Rs. 35 per yard. It was the first day in my life that I had got sewn such an expensive and imported cloth. I wore it the entire day. I was ready after putting on my clothes when my companion came and started getting ready, because he had to buy a suit. After having breakfast with them, we went to the market to buy suits. Bought a suit in about two hours. Its cost had to be paid 51 dollars, in those days it was 175 rupees. Today it is even more. Our 4 Rupees 14 Annas is equal to one dollar here. But here the cost of the suits is lesser than it is in our India. The fabrics here are also very good. The suits are also very well stitched. I bought about 5 suits from here which lasted for about 5 years.

When we came back to the room after buying a suit, my friend wore it but he did not know how to put on a tie. This poor person tried again and again but could not tie it properly. He asked for my help but even I didn't know much about it.

I learned to tie a tie from my friend while coming to America because earlier in life I had never felt the need to tie a tie and neither had I wanted to. I still could not understand the importance of tying a tie. I consider it a very stupid thing. But I always go out here wearing a tie. Because that's the custom here. You must have heard an English proverb: Do in Rome as Romans do. I helped him and the knot of the tie was somewhat satisfactory this time. He also used to consider tying a tie a trouble. The poor man was so puzzled that whenever he used to take off the shirt, he used to loosen the knot of the tie a little only and let it remain in the collar itself so that he would not have to tie it again. It was also great fun to talk about his tie.

This day was September 11th. In the evening we had to go to Berkeley to attend a reception organised by the Government of India and the University of California. Berkeley was quite far from our hotel. But the hoteliers and the Education Secretary of the Government of India had well explained the way to go there. But the reception was at 7 o'clock in the evening and there was all day left. Where should I go? The hoteliers suggested to us why not to take a tourist bus and see the historic and other prominent buildings of the city of San Francisco. The suggestion was very kind and welcome. We started in a group of about eight towards the tourist bus-station. The way was not known, but we managed to reach it by asking. The tourist guides were also used to stand on the tourist buses. One of them rushed towards us and asked us what we wanted to see. They had two types of tourists. One for half a day and the other for the full day. The fare was also according to it. We decided to take a half day tour. I can't remember exactly what we had to pay. But it did not exceed ten dollars (50 rupees). The tourist guide also arranged for our tickets and we boarded the bus at 9:30 hrs. There were other passengers too on the bus, most of whom were Americans. Just after 9:30am the bus started.

Maybe you want to know about the buses here, so I am writing. Here because the population is less, the labour is very expensive and it is five times that of India. The buses here have also been made keeping this vision in front. That is, there is only one man in these buses. He is a driver, conductor and ticket distributor at the same time. The door to board the bus is with the driver and the door to get down is right in the middle of the bus which opens only when the driver presses the button while sitting in his seat. This work is done in seconds and the passengers are also helpful. No one travels here without a ticket. You might be surprised to know that the buses and cars here run about 45 miles per hour. That's why every week about 576 deaths are caused by motor accidents. The buses here are very comfortable and air conditioned.

As soon as the bus started moving, the driver introduced the general plan of the journey to the passengers through the microphone. He used to talk about the good places which came on the way. But the place, which was special, we used to get down from the bus and the driver used to tell us about these places. We went to San Francisco's museum, zoo and many historical places. When our bus came to a hill, the whole city of San Francisco was visible from there. One of the biggest bridges of the sea and the world, the Golden Bridge also seemed to be very good. Apart from the historical places, we went to a big garden here, where there were hundreds of beautiful flowers of various kinds. The climate of San Francisco is considered very well. Snow falls here occasionally, but the weather always remains the same as it happens in the month of December in Delhi. We roamed for five hours. After this our bus came back and stopped from where it had left at 2:30pm.

It would be around 3 o'clock. We felt a little hungry and decided to eat something. There was a place to eat nearby. I ate a sandwich. You may ask what a sandwich is. Here the sandwich is very common. It is of many types. There is also meat, cheese and tomato too. I only ate tomatoes. It is very easy to make this. It is made by placing tomato and lettuce leaves between two pieces of bread. Butter is also applied. Maybe you remember once or twice I had prepared and ate it in front of you in Delhi. Here at lunch, mostly the sandwiches are eaten. After having some food, we started towards our hotel.

Coming into the room, I laid down for a while and for some time my eyes were also fixed. When I woke up it was 5 o'clock. Washing my face, I got ready and went to the hotel reception with my friends to attend the reception at Berkeley. We were about to go out when we came to know that Mr. *Muhammad Ali Jinnah* had died. Sad to hear. It was even more saddened when the hoteliers said that there would be a nice feast to celebrate the death of Mr. Jinnah. That's why after the meeting, we should come here and eat food. I didn't like this idea at all. But food was food. Whether in this hotel or in any outside hotel. We headed to Berkeley and got there before 7 o'clock. There, at first condolence was expressed on the death of Mr. Jinnah. To which some students raised objections who had suffered the loss of the partition of India. The debate took a serious turn. But an old American professor intervened. After a while the meeting ended, we went to our respective hotels after meeting the students of some other countries.

On reaching the Goldfield Hotel, we got Gujarati style food. One *paratha* was also given at the same time. The food was very tasty. But I did not like the occasion in which it was made. Once it came to mind that food should not be eaten here. But it was so late in the night that there was doubt whether food would be available elsewhere or not. Apart from this, I was not even aware of this new place. Helplessly, I had to eat there. After having dinner, we came to the drawing room of the hotel and started talking about Mr. Jinnah and the politics of India. A lot has been said against the partition of India. Some old revolutionaries were also sitting there. They also narrated their own stories, and *Gandhiji* and many other leaders were accused of creating Pakistan. You know the history of our freedom struggle. You will remember that these revolutionaries had fled from India here in the partition of Bengal in 1908 and after 1912. Here they had formed a Gadar party and used to run the national movement of India sitting from America itself. I hold a different view from their point of view. Because it has been and will be my belief that non-violence is the only means by which any enemy can be conquered. Our conversation went on till about 1 o'clock in the night, then we went to our respective rooms to sleep.

When I woke up in the morning, it was 8 o'clock. My friend was still sleeping. He too must have got up by about 8:30. By 8:30, I got ready and after breakfast started writing some letters. After writing letters, I made a program for the whole day with my friend. It was also decided when and by which train we should go towards Ann Arbour. While we were discussing only, I got a telephone call from the Secretary of the Embassy of India that the Government of India has secured a vehicle for Indian students for tomorrow evening and in that vehicle, the students who came in the "S.S. General Meags" will go to their respective universities. He also said that those who are not on the scholarship of the Government of India should buy their tickets.

All of us who were staying at the Goldfield Hotel were not on scholarship from the Government of India. That's why we discussed why not do this auspicious work now. I walked towards the railway station with three more companions and reached there in about 20 minutes. The fare from San Francisco to Ann Arbour was about $50 (Rs 250) This was the fare for coach class. I have already written that there are two classes in the train - one is Coach and the other is Pullman. After buying tickets, we took a walk through the market and then came back to our hotel.

The next day we had to leave the hotel and go to Ann Arbour, so I wrote a few more letters. Packed things up and went for a walk. Came back in the afternoon, sat for a while. Noted addresses from the people and then came to the railway station in the evening to catch the train.

American trains are different from Indian trains in many ways. The trains here are air-conditioned and the coaches are tall, which are often connected to each other. This makes it easy to move from one compartment to another. Coach class fares are cheaper than Pullman. The seats are very comfortable and one can sleep even on them easily. These seats are not like our trains, but like we have "*Aaram Kursi*" (Comfy chair) in our place. These comfy chairs can also be stretched while sleeping. There are lower and upper berths in the Pullman class. This class is very expensive and its seats are like our first class. But the Pullman class here is considered better than any other trains in the world. I have travelled in both Coach and Pullman. Not with my own money, but I travelled in this class once when I was a Fellow of the Rockefeller Foundation, on its scholarship. I liked it a lot. Usually the speed of these trains is 80 to 85 miles per hour. At first I did not believe that the trains could run so fast, but when I sat on the train and counted the electric poles passing by outside myself, I was somewhat convinced. Some trains also have observatories, that is, there is a two-storey compartment above the rail, in which one can sit and watch the scenery outside. This compartment is also air conditioned and its roof is made of moncelight glass roof). Sitting in this observatory, I saw the beautiful hills of Colorado. It took us three days from San Francisco to Ann Arbour. There was also a dining car for food, but I had kept a lot of fruits with me. I had been taking some food on the way as well. Apart from the dining car in the train, sandwiches, milk, coffee and food items were available on the seats only, because all these items used to be sold by the railway staff itself. To see what the dining room here looks like, I went there to get breakfast once.

When our train was passing through the mountains and caves, it seemed to be very nice. Some caves were more than a mile long. The mountains of Colorado used to look very beautiful. I had also purchased some pictures there, which I had brought with me. All these pictures are in Delhi. I will show you when I return to India. After the city of Salt Lake, when our train headed towards Chicago, a large green area started. Corn fields were visible for miles. Wherever you looked, it was green and green. I will never forget this first and longest train journey of my life.

It was a lot of fun along the way. The compartment in which I was sitting was reserved for Indian students only. But as our train got closer to Ann Arbour, the number of companions kept decreasing. Eight of us students had to go to Ann Arbour. That is why these eight students remained along till the end. After reaching Chicago, we changed to another train to Ann Arbour and arrived at Ann Arbour station at 6 pm. From there, we took taxis to the centre of international students.

8

First 10 months in Ann Arbour

After a long time, today I am sitting again to tell you this story. You already know how busy I have been in my studies in the last months. After working hard day and night for almost two years, I was able to finish my thesis and pass the examination. I am working hard nowadays as well. I do practical training all day. At 10 o'clock in the night and even on Saturdays and Sundays, I am collecting material for my book on *Pt. Nehru*.

I think that when I come to India, I should publish my thesis which is on *Gandhiji* and this book too which is on *Pt. Nehru*. Let us see what God approves. I have already written this in my earlier letters that to achieve true success in life, man must do years of hard work and sacrifice. I want to become such a successful person in my life so that I can do something for other creatures of the world. Everyone fills their own stomach. Are you not my other hand Prem? My success is your success and your success is mine.

In the earlier letter, I had written to you about the condition of my arrival to Ann Arbour and that when our team came to Ann Arbour, accommodation had not been arranged. All the rooms in Ann Arbour were full because that year more students had come than ever before. The biggest reason for this can be said that Clare Veterkas, was supported by the US Government providing payment of all the expenses for studying and buying books, under the GI Bill. They have taken admission in universities again. There were a large number of foreign students too.

When we could not find any place to stay, temporary beds were set up in the International Centre itself and we slept there for three to four days. Perhaps on the fifth day we were told that the village of Willoran, about 20 miles from Ann Arbour, accommodations had been found in a war-time residence. These accommodations were built for the craftsmen working in the aeroplane factory during the days of the war. These (dormitories) were made during Second World War and were clean and tidy.

There were many dormitories here and about 2,000 students lived in them. There were university buses to take us to and from the university, which used to arrive every thirty minutes.

Classes in American universities start at 8 o'clock in the morning and go on until the evening. This does not mean that the students stay in the classes all day, but the student who has taken admission goes to that class on time. The big advantage of this is that here students keep earning and keep studying. It is not so in India. I took my first class at eight in the morning. I had to take the bus at 7 o'clock to join the class exactly at 8 o'clock. By 7:30 hrs we used to reach the bus station which was near our general library. There was a snack shop near the bus station, where I used to have hot coffee and snack before reaching my class five minutes ahead of time. Since American universities are different from Indian universities, so it was not only strange for me but rather at start it was difficult too. I didn't understand many things. Every week exams are held here. After the start of my studies, I also took the test, so I could not write the correct answers. I went to my professor and explained the reason why the questions did not make sense to me. The professor politely asked me to read the question carefully next week and also told me to read the books carefully. I followed the same and then started scoring good marks in all the further exams.

All the libraries here are open from 8 o'clock in the morning to 10 o'clock in the night, students often study in the libraries only. There is no such custom in India yet. Each school and department of the university has its own separate library. Not only is the library of our department separate, but every student has an individual table, which is allotted to him every semester. This makes studies very easy. I used to come at eight in the morning and go back by bus at 10:30 in the night. After studying for an hour, I used to sleep after 12 o'clock so that I could easily wake up at 6 o'clock in the morning.

There were about 100 students in the dormitory in which I lived. Of these, 8 were Indians. The rest were either Americans or foreigners. My room was two-seater and I had to pay $28 per month as rent. My roommate was a Muslim from Bombay. His name was *Shoji Hydari* and was a very warm-hearted man. There was a dentist from Punjab in a single occupancy room near my room. In the room in front of me, there was a professor from

Bihar and a brother from Mathura (Sohan Lal Sharma). Both of them were students of psychology. Almost all the students of our team of 1948 are gone. Many of them have completed Ph.D.

The son of a big businessman of Bombay also lived in this dormitory. Sometimes we used to sit together and talk and sing songs too.

Life was tough those days. I had to work so hard that it was not known where the sun rose and where it set. It was getting cold and it was snowing too much. This was the first time in my life that I had seen snow fall. It was a beautiful sight. The cafeteria near the dormitories was also closed during the Christmas holidays. The city was far away. Bus service was also reduced. One day brother of Bihar came up with a solution that an electric heater should be bought and vegetables can be prepared in the room itself. His suggestion was very nice and we all accepted it. During Christmas holidays, we used to make vegetables of potatoes, peas, *aloo gobi* etc. and used to drink milk after eating it with bread. This way the holidays during the Christmas passed. After the opening of the cafeteria, we started eating food there itself.

Maybe you want to ask what the meaning of the word cafeteria is. The cafeteria system is now running in India too. The best example of this is "Annapurna" which has now opened in Delhi, Bombay, and Calcutta etc. It can neither be called a restaurant nor a hotel, but it is a place to eat where people stand in a line and pick up the food items from the window themselves which they want to eat. Then give the price of those things to the cashier sitting at the counter and lift their own saucers and sit on the table and chair lying in the cafeteria. After eating food, in some cafeterias, they pick up the saucers themselves and put them on a big table and in some cafeterias leave them on the table itself. In the Michigan Union we had to pick up our own saucers and put them on a large table in a corner. One day, while I was having dinner at the Michigan Union, I myself was introduced to an American student. In conversation, I asked him what you want to become in your life. He was a good poet and writer. I liked his ideas because in the materialistic society of America, only one or two among thousands would like to make this the purpose of their life. We became very familiar and he started reciting his poems. I could not hold either. I also revealed one day that I too have a great passion for poetry and sometimes I write too. It was just a delay of revealing it and he asked me to recite my poems and I had to recite it.

I would have been introduced to this American poet about two months before December. On Christmas he presented me with a collection of poems by an American poet. The name of the poet is Walter Whitman (1819–1892) and the name of this book is Leaves of Grass (1855). This poet wrote a book, Passage to India (1871). I liked this poet very much. It is said that Americans did not like him that much. This poet friend not only presented this book but also invited me to visit his home for the Christmas feast. His home is in Jackson, a town near Ann Arbour. His father came to pick us up and dropped me at my residence after dinner. He also took pictures with me near the Christmas tree, which I will show you. This friend has been so influenced by Indian civilization that he has started studying Vedanta in *Ramakrishna* Mission and perhaps may have gone to India now. There he would teach at the University of Calcutta and also study Vedanta. He had given this information to me in a letter which he had sent to me about five months ago.

When I returned from New York to attend a conference in Ann Arbour in 1950, I sent a special letter to this friend. He answered immediately. I had to go to New York after four days to attend the conference. This friend came to meet me at the railway station and presented me with beautiful flowers.

When I moved from India to America in 1948, I was a very skinny boy, but after coming here, at the end of December I realised that my clothes were getting smaller. There were no dollars to buy new suits. I decided to get my two suits altered which I had brought from India. To get them altered, I had to pay 12 dollars to the tailor i.e. about 60 rupees. The standard of living here is four times more than our standard of living.

During these days I was also invited to visit two churches and had the opportunity to talk to many Christian friends. For Thanksgiving Day, which is a big festival here, I got an invitation from an American farmer. The farmer came to pick me up at my house in his car and took me to his farm, which would be about 12 miles from Ann Arbour. A farmer of America is different from Indian farmers. The American farmer has at least two cars, one or two trucks, tractors and many such big things. Its house is also like that of an urban dweller of any city. Its house has a telephone, television, newspapers, loungers, carpets and a small library. They often grow their own food. They also raise chickens and do the work themselves for their own comfort. Some farmers even have their own aircraft. This was my first time seeing an American farmer. But there is poverty here too. I will write about it sometime soon.

I took my examinations at the end of January 1949 and by the grace of God passed in all subjects. My scores were also very good. The spring studies started from mid-February and it ended in the first week of June because I already had three bachelor's degrees, so I did A.M.L.S in June itself. Perhaps the convocation was on June 15th. I attended it dressed in full academic attire and took my A.M.L.S. degree. A *Bengali* friend of mine who used to take very good photos also took pictures of the occasion which I have in Delhi. I will show you when I come back.

In the first week of March, while I was sitting at Michigan Union with two of my American friends over coffee, one of them asked what I would do after June. I said that I will go back to India. He again asked if I would not take practical training. I said "Where?" He said that in the Library of Congress, Washington D.C. I started thinking about who would give me a chance to give practical training and fell silent thinking about this. The next day while we were again having coffee at that time, the same friend asked if I had sent an application to the Library of Congress. I said no. So he said that there is no harm in submitting the application. At least send the application form.

During the same week, the head of our librarianship department received a letter from the United Nations saying that the students studying library science in your school should, if they choose to work in the United Nations library, fill out the application as soon as possible. My name was also in this letter. I was called by the chairman and asked if I would like to work in the U. N. library. I said, "with great pleasure". I filled up the application and sent it to the Speaker along with my letter attached.

Two weeks later, a letter arrived from the Library of Congress and the Library of the United Nations, and to my delight, I got the opportunity to learn the work at both places. I consulted my professor about where it would be best for me to go. He asked me to go to the Library of Congress. I decided to go to the Library of Congress first, and after two months to the United Nations Library. I also wrote to the United Nations Library. I was to start work in the Library of Congress on July 1. Taking a degree at the convocation ceremony on June 15, at five o'clock in the evening on June 17, I started towards Washington DC which is the capital of America and reached there in the morning on 18th June.

Here I feel it appropriate to write that my views on American society as of 1950 were not the same as they were in June 1948. And even today they are not. I will write about this in full detail in my last chapter. But at this time I will write in brief.

In America in the beginning, I used to see everyone as God. In all the letters I wrote in those days, I expressed such thoughts that there are no people who are true, direct and great friendly like the people of America. Compared the society here with heaven, but as soon as I saw this society from close range, I talked to these people in a mixed way, there was no limit to the surprise and I started thinking in my mind that there is no special quality in these people. They are also like other people of the world, they have bad and good ones, like all other human beings in the world.

The biggest difference that I see between my people and them is that these people are very materialistic, and we mostly believe in spiritualism. The parents here do not treat their children like we do. Their relations are mostly materialistic. The owner of the house in which I live takes house rent from her son like me, cooks food separately from her son, etc. There are many such examples. Sons and daughters all behave like this to their parents. The matter of relatives is completely different. They might be as if they don't even exist. But we don't have such things at our place. There are many other things here which are different from our society. I would say that our civilization is millions of standards better than their civilization. Yes, it has to be said that America has made more technological progress than us, but the spiritual speed is not there for even a small amount.

We Indian students become victims of some materialistic environment here. But a true and sincere Indian tries to learn from here only those things which are right for him. This is the reason why some students keep wasting their time here. They don't study. Years go by that they do not pass the exam. They work just to earn bread. But we should remain like a lotus in water. Above water even after being in water. What we have to learn from here, we have to learn it and return to our country as soon as possible so that we too can help in making our country a great country in the world. In my words, Americans still have a lot to learn from us and we have to learn from them in the technical field; this I agree. In the next letter, I will write about the University of Michigan and the state of Michigan. Keep this chapter safe with you as well.

9

Glimpse of Michigan University and State of Michigan

The University of Michigan was founded in 1817 in the city of Detroit, about 35 miles from Ann Arbour. Initially its name was University of Michigan. When Michigan State became a member of the United States Union, an act of March 20, 1837, established the University of Michigan in Ann Arbour. The buildings of the university started being built and after a few days, the studies also started. Its first class had seven students and the number of professors was three. But while progressing, today the number of its students is about 23,000, out of which about 1,100 scholars have come from almost all the countries of the world to get higher education. The number of Indian students is about 65. There are 18 big schools in this university and there are 35 departments in these schools in which the same number of subjects are taught. The university is spread over several miles. Its number of big buildings is about 45.

The General Library here is considered to be the eighth largest library in the country. It contains 856,810 books. The number of maps is 62,000. It opens at eight in the morning and closes at 10 in the night. Besides the General Library, there are twenty departmental libraries. The university has three museums. There are big fields for playing and there are lakes for swimming. The University of Michigan Stadium is one of the largest stadiums in the country. It can seat 67,000 people. The university has its own hospital. There is also a Department of Health Services, in which every student is thoroughly checked before admission. Every student has to stand naked in the line. And every part of his body is carefully observed by the doctors. I was also examined for about two and a half hours.

There is an international centre for foreign students, where there is a good arrangement to sit and play. Nearby is the 'Michigan Union' where most of the men eat. Most girls eat in the 'Michigan League' but there is co-education. And boys and girls sit together and study.

The university also offers many scholarships and fellowships. Most of the students keep studying here and also do part time jobs to meet their expenses. Foreigners have to seek permission from immigration authorities before starting to work here.

Students also live here in many ways—some in dormitories, some in residence halls and some in private homes. I live in a private house on rent. The university has its own powerhouse. The heating system is also its own. The method of doing hot water is different, due to which hot water comes round the clock in the taps. The university has its own private police and the rules and regulations are also their own. There is a small market near the university, which is called campus here. Ann Arbour is a small town. Its population is 29,815. The city is small but clean. The roads are wide. The houses are not very high, but there are definitely five to six storeys.

There are trees everywhere, there is green grass and there are clean tracks of cement. Music concerts are very often here. There are plays too. Great speakers also have speeches. Dr *Radhakrishnan* of India has also been invited to deliver a speech in the coming fall session. Mrs. *Vijaya-lakshmi Pandit* also gave a speech here. Mr. *Mehta,* who is presently the Ambassador of India, had come last year to deliver a speech. Michigan University is the largest university in America. Its standard is very high.

After knowing about the Michigan University and the education system there, you would like to have some information about the state of Michigan as well. American Indians lived in this state before the Americans. The name Michigan was also given by them. In 1618, the people of France defeated the American Indians and established their kingdom. After this, the British also started coming and took possession of a large part of this state. But the American Indians did not like the British. They fought against the British but could not win. After the American Revolution (1775-83), the Americans won the State of Michigan in the battle that took place between the Americans and the British.

The area of this state is 58,216 square miles, of which 1,194 square miles are many lakes. The population of this state was 6,371,766 according to the 1950 census. In terms of population, the status of this state is seventh in America. This state is considered to be a large, rich, and happy state. There are many large factories in the state of Michigan. Here milk, curd, fruits etc. are in abundance. It is the hub of the automobile industry. More cars and aeroplanes are made here than in all countries of the world. World famous car models are manufactured here. I remember when I went to Detroit in December 1948 to see the Ford Assembly Live, 35 miles from Ann Arbour, I was surprised to see two cars coming out after every minute, like a potter making a toy and keeping it aside. Thousands of men and women work in Ford Assembly Live. The factory of 'General Motors' is also here.

The coloured photo I sent with Dr Swami was taken on the banks of the Detroit River. Michigan and Canada are close by. Only the Detroit River separates them. The names of the big cities of the state of Michigan are- Detroit, Dearborn, Flint, East Lansing, Grand Rapids, Battle Creek, Jackson etc. East Lansing is the capital of this state.

There are large lakes in this State and there are many forests too. Ann Arbour is known for lakes, forests and greenery all around. It is very cold here too. Michigan Lake, which is 307 miles long and 118 miles wide, is the third largest in America. It is 579.79 feet high above the sea. Very large ships also run in this lake, in which goods are often brought and taken from here. I like both the University of Michigan and the state of Michigan. But no country in the world is as dear to me as I love my country. This statement is also true – "*Janani Janmabhoomi, Swargadapi Gariyasi*" (mother and motherland are superior even to heaven).

In the next letter I will write about my stay in Washington DC.

10

Departure from Ann Arbour to Washington and Training at the Library of Congress

927 Sylvan Avenue
NR class
Michigan (U.S.A.)
Date July 10, 1954.

I have written in the eighth letter that I had decided not to go to the United Nations and take two months practical training in the Library of Congress. The biggest reason for this was that the Library of Congress is the largest library in the world. Therefore, getting training in this would be very beneficial. After this I had intended to go to the United Nations library.

I left for Washington D.C. on the evening of June 17,1949 by the 5:30 pm train. At about 4 p.m. few close friends of mine took group photos on the steps of the University of Michigan General Library, which Mr. Bagchi had sent me after I moved to Washington. I have those pictures, I'll show you. After taking pictures we went to Michigan Union and after drinking coffee. They came home with me and from there they came to drop me off at the station with my luggage.

It is only natural that I felt something while leaving Ann Arbour; But when I reached Washington and started working, everything was normalised. I reached Washington D.C. in the morning. I had already made arrangements to stay there in the International Home by writing a letter to them.

The training in the Library of Congress was to start from July 1. I had two weeks to travel. In these two weeks, I visited a lot of places in Washington D.C. which is the capital of America. Maybe you want to know a little more about Washington DC, so I will write some special things.

Washington DC is the capital of America. According to the census of 1940, its population is 663,091. Its population in 1948 was approximately

863,000. The foundation of this city was laid in 1762 and its map maker was Pierre L'enfant. The foundation of the President's White House was also laid in the same year and the construction of the Capitol Building began in 1793. The first meeting of the American Congress was held in this city in 1800 and elected Thomas Jefferson as America's first president in Washington DC. In 1814 the British ransacked the city and set the President's White House on fire; But then gradually its condition started improving. The American Civil War also hindered its progress a lot. But after the defeat of the Confederates, it began to progress without any hindrance. Within a few years, this city spread over 70 square miles and beautiful buildings, gardens, gardens started being built. These are the major parks of Washington DC – Potomac, Rock Creek, Anacostia and National Geological Park. The names of the big buildings here are- Capital Building where the meetings of Congress and Senate are held; Library of Congress which is the largest library in the world; The Folger Shakespeare Memorial Library, the largest Shakespeare library in the world, is made of marble; National Archaeological Museum building; Here I received a mass practical training in 1950; The Constitutional Hall, the Supreme Court Building, the National Gallery of Art and the Pentagon which is the largest war office in the world. I went here too to see photo duplication machines in connection with my practical training. Along with this, the buildings of Corcoran Gallery of Art, Walter Reed Hospital and U.S. Naval Observatory are prominent.

Since Washington DC is the capital of America, there are many statues and national monuments here. Famous among them are the Washington Memorial, the Lincoln Memorial and the Thomas Jefferson Memorial. In the memory of the soldiers who died in the First and Second World War, Arlington National Cemetery is worth seeing. A friend of mine took a picture of me here that is also with me.

कोलम्बिया विश्वविद्यालय
Columbia University

There are also many large educational institutions and universities in Washington DC. Their names are- America Georgetown University, George Washington University, and Howard University which belongs to the Negro people, Smithsonian Institution, Brookings Institution, Carnegie Institution of Washington, and American University.

From June 18th to 30th, I was engrossed in seeing these large buildings and educational institutions of Washington DC. I saw them walking, sitting in the bus and getting into friends' cars. Let me tell an interesting story here. On the afternoon of June 18, when I was looking at the Capitol Building, I met a couple. They got married recently. The husband was a medical doctor, and the wife was a Spanish girl. The wife asked me whether I had come from India. I said yes. Then she asked if I knew *Nayan Nara Pandit*? I said personally no, but I have definitely heard the name. Then she started saying that I was her classmate when she studied there. This couple were very respectful. They took me in their car for two days and showed me almost all the big buildings in Washington DC. The husband was an officer in the Dr Veteran's Hospital. Once he invited me to come to the Catholic Church and also introduced me to his mother-in-law and friends.

I also went to my embassy (Indian Embassy) In those days Mrs. *Vijayalakshmi Pandit* was the Indian Ambassador. I met her too.

Two weeks passed while roaming like this. My training started in the Library of Congress from 1st July. On the first day a film was shown to all the trainees to tell them about the 'Library of Congress' and then I was introduced to the head of each section and department, and I got some information about their departments. But most of my time was spent in the 'India section' of 'Orientalia Division'. My Head was Dr Paulman who was also the Cultural Attaché in New Delhi from 1950 to 1952. He is a very noble and virtuous person and is fully acquainted with Indian literature and civilization. I learned a lot in his section. [1]

On 31st August my training ended at the Library of Congress. After this I got the golden opportunity to manage the library of the 'Information-Services-Department,' of the Embassy of India. It was only two months after I came here that the United Nations wrote to me if I wanted to come there, I should inform them soon. I thought why not go to the United Nations. I asked for leave for two months; but how to get leave, only two months

---

1. On the retirement of Dr. Humel Paulman has now become the President of the 'Orientalia Division'.

ago I started working here. The desire to go to the United Nations grew so much that I resigned in a hurry and went to the United Nations to take practical training.

Had I not resigned from the Indian Embassy, it may have been possible that today there would have been an officer in the Foreign Service. But I do not regret, maybe God had given me that opportunity to do other great work, due to which I could do PhD and I kept getting inspired to work continuously.

In these four months I also worked on 'Gandhi-Bibliography'. After office hours, I used to work on it for about three hours daily. I got it typed in November before I left Washington, and the manuscript was 250 pages.

During these days I stayed in the International Building. It is a small 'International Building'; but there were students from almost all the countries of the world. Every Friday there was some function or the other. There were dances too. But I had never learned to dance; that's why I didn't even have to participate in it. I have not learned to dance till today, what will I learn now? There was a small garden in this building in which there was a peach tree.

This tree used to have very good Kashmir peaches, which we used to eat too. The director of this building was an Englishman. He had a little boy named Johnny. He was a very sweet child. I used to play with him sometimes. We used to go out of town on picnics sometimes. Everyone used to take their own food there and used to eat while sitting on the banks of the river.

There is no Indian restaurant in Washington DC but there is a Baghdad restaurant. There was an Indian type of khichdi (rice and lentil). Sometimes I used to go to eat it. Sometimes I was invited by friends who had cooking facilities with them. We used to eat together after preparing Indian food. Finding Indian food in America was like something precious has been found.

On 31 October I left Washington and from 1 November started working in the United Nations, Lake Access, New York. I will write about it in the next letter. Keep it safe. I was there when *Pt Nehru* came to Washington DC. I went to the airport to pick him up along with others from the Embassy. I have many of his pictures which were captured.

11

Two Months in Lake Success

I had left Washington D.C. on the evening of October 31 and arrived in New York just after midnight; Because it takes only about 6 hours to reach here by bus. Lake Success is about 25 miles from New York, where the first UN office was located. I wanted to live near Lake Success instead of living in New York. So I started living in Great Neck, a small town about 30 miles away from New York and very close to Lake Success. There used to be other people working in U.N. Daily United Nations buses used to take us and drop us back in the evening. In Great Neck I lived on Second Avenue. This place will be about half a mile away from the bus and railway stations. My landlord's name was Shreyut Green. This house was very large and there was a garden nearby. These people were very friendly and happy. Two foreigners working in the United Nations also lived in this house.

I started practical training as a trainee from 2nd November. Interns or trainees are those who finish their studies and get practical experience somewhere. I happened to get this opportunity only for two months and I used to get 250 dollars each month which was too much for me. I was trained here in all aspects. But spent much of his time in the reference department of the UN Library. I was learning to work under an Englishman and his name was Mr. Roberts. He was a great man and I learned a lot from him.

You must ask me what is the UN? What is its purpose, why was its foundation laid and who started it? I am writing its short story below. The international organisation United Nations was formed soon after the Second World War in place of 'League of Nations'. The United Nations was created by President F.D. Roosevelt in 1941 with countries fighting against Asia. Its legal work began on January 1, 1941, when 26 nations joined the United

Nations Declaration and pledged to continue the war proceedings together instead of separate reconciliations.

The need to replace the league with an international organisation was felt first on 30 October 1943 in the Moscow Declaration, published by China, Great Britain, the United States and Russia. In the Dumberlane Conference under Great Britain (February 4 to 11, 1945) the United States and Russia agreement was rejected – by a vote in the Security Council.

At the Yalta Conference, it was decided to organise a conference of all the states, which was finally included in the declaration of the United Nations of 1942 and which declared war on either Germany or Japan from March 1st, 1945.

Many countries also made declarations of war and thus became legal for the conference to be held in San Francisco from 25 April to 26 June 1945. Initially 46 nations participated. It had already been decided to include Argentina, Valarsa, Ukraine and Denmark which had just been liberated. Of these 51 original members, a place was also reserved for Poland, which could not participate due to a dispute over a responsible government. The remaining original members were Australia, Belgium, Bolivia, Brazil, Canada, Chile, China, Colombia, Costa Rica, Cuba, Czechoslovakia, the Ecuadorian Republic, Egypt, Ethiopia, France, Greece, Guatemala, Haiti, Honduras, India, Iraq, Iran, Lebanon, Liberia, Lemberg, Mexico, the Netherlands, New Zealand, Nicaragua, Norway, Panama, Paraguay, Peru, Philippines, Saudi Arabia, Syria, Turkey, Union of South Africa, Soviet Republic, United Kingdom, United States, Uruguay, Venezuela and Yugoslavia.

Other nations that were included later were Afghanistan, Burma, Iceland, Israel, Pakistan, Sweden, Thailand, and Yemen. The San Francisco Conference created the Administrative Treaty and the United Nations Charter. It was signed on 26 June and was deemed to have been passed by the required states on 24 October which is also known as UN Day.

The first meeting of the General Assembly was held in London on 10 January 1946 and two days later the first meeting of the Security Council was convened. It was decided that the office of the United Nations should be kept in the United States. In December 1946, the General Assembly accepted John D. Rockefeller's offer of 42,000,000 rupees to purchase a piece of land along the East River near Manhattan to make a permanent office which was temporarily in the Parliament. At present, the permanent head office of the United Nations is in New York.

The purpose of the United Nations is to establish world peace and security, to develop mutual friendship among states and to obtain cooperation in solving international economic, social, cultural, and human problems.

What I have written above about the United Nations is very little. Many books have been written on this and more will be written; But these words will give you some idea about this organisation. The objectives for which its foundation was laid, today it is seen that it is only a hope. I was there when the War of Korea started in 1950. India did not participate in the United Nations. My faith too was shaken from then on by the purposes of the United Nations. Yes, the United Nations has helped a lot in publishing and interpreting the civilizations, history and literature of the countries of the world. Today the question before the United Nations is whether to accept Red China or not. America doesn't want that. The rest of the countries want it. According to last week's news, America's big politicians said that if the United Nations accepts Red China, then they will separate themselves from the United Nations. This means that the United Nations should run under the policies of America, otherwise it does not exist. It is also correct; The US provides more than half the cost of the United Nations. I will talk about the United Nations in detail later.

संयुक्त राष्ट्रसंघ का भवन

Office of the United Nations

In the first two months, I went to the General Assembly of the United Nations and to the meetings of the Security Council. This experience was also unique. Many times I attended cultural evenings. Every week one or the other country displayed its civilization. There was a snack room here. Every country's food was cooked there. I used to eat lunch there only. Here only I got introduced to Late *Shri Narasimha Rao* of India, *R.K.R.U. Rao*, Dr *Mudaliar*, Dr *Kumarappa*, Mrs *Sucheta* etc.

My two months internship ended on 31st December; But I got the membership of Rockefeller Foundation for the next 6 months. I will write about it in the next letter.

12

Tourism as a member of the Rockefeller Foundation

927 Sylvan Avenue
NR class
Michigan (U.S.A.)
Date August 03, 1954

On December 20, 1949, in the afternoon I received the good news that I had been selected as a member of the Rockefeller Foundation. I got this news from the Director of the Library of the United Nations, Dr Milam. I was very happy to hear this. Because being a fellow of this foundation is not an easy thing. I had already been interviewed for this fellowship two weeks ago, but I was not expecting much. I got this membership for only six months i.e. from 1st January to 30th June 1949. According to this, I used to get $175 per month, first class train fare for the journey and hotel accommodation, i.e. about $250 or (Rs. 1,250) per month. I did not spend the total amount, whichever was left, I took it back to India. Converted it to Rupees, which was about 8,000 rupees.

On the evening of 24 December, there was a Christmas party in the United Nations. I attended it along with the entire staff of the UN Library. I remember that the assistant director of the UN Library, a librarian from France, introduced me to other people and told me that I am his adopted son, and he is learning to work in our library and is a member of Rockefeller. Everyone was happy knowing this.

When I was studying in the United Nations, I lived on Second Arch in the town of Great Neck, near Lake Success. This place is about ten miles away from Lake Success. I used to come and go to U.N. in the morning and evening by the bus itself. Many UN employees lived here. Those who had their own cars used to come and go by cars and those who did not have cars used to come and go in buses only. Great-Neck is about 40 miles from New York. Whenever I had to go to New York, I used to go by Long Island electric train. This train used to stop at small stations and took about 35 minutes.

The house at Great Neck was also very nice. I lived on the third floor of this house. Some days I also cooked food there. Sometimes used to make spinach greens and potatoes, peas etc. and used to drink hot milk with bread. One day *puris* were also made, but they became big. Every Saturday and Sunday evening, after cooking and eating, I used to go to the movies and used to sit there for about four hours. You would know that here the movie starts at 11 o'clock and ends at 12 or 1 in the night. Somebody can come anytime and sit. It is not a custom like India to come on time when the film starts and everyone has to leave the hall when the film ends. All the movie houses here are air conditioned. They are cold in summer and warm in winter and has only one class. Anyone can sit anywhere with a ticket. Upstairs in the gallery or downstairs in the front seat or in the back seat. In our country, there are many classes in cinema.

If I used to get hungry after watching the picture at night, I used to eat ice cream. In those days I was very fond of 'Banana Slit ice cream'. My stomach used to get full as soon as I used to eat it. Also used to eat 'grilled sandwich'. Then I used to come and sleep. Because even in those days I was working on the same book which I have now finished for my PhD. I used to get less time due to excessive work and in the time I got, I either used to watch movies or museums in New York etc.

All the days I lived in the United Nations; my life was very beautiful. There was an opportunity to meet the leaders of every country. Heard their speeches in the Security Council and the General Assembly. Every evening a film was shown on the cultural customs and civilization of one or the other country. Wherever I used to go, there was great respect.

In those days there was a volunteer service in the United Nations. Invitations used to come from American organisations and private individuals in this department. Invitations also came to me many times but due to more work, I could not accept all the invitations; But went out three times. Once I went to Harishdung during Christmas days. The second time I went to a town near New York. And the third time I was with an American farmer. These people are very hospitable; But now they are turning against India. You know the reason. But India has always been an advocate of peace and will remain so. We don't have to fight with anyone and we don't have to join hands with those who fight.

There were about 50 more Indians in the United Nations. Sir *Bengal Rao* was the chief representative those days. His staff was also substantially mainly Indians. Two of them were my dear friends too. One had come from Delhi only, who used to study in 'Naidu College' at some point of time . He was here with his wife and they also had two little sons. Many times he invited me to his house for dinner. Nowadays he is a senior officer of the Government of India. Apart from this, there was also a Bengali brother. He is also in India nowadays.

About 20 countries used to work in the United Nations Library. It felt very international to meet all of them and work with them at one place. I can say that working in the United Nations has greatly enhanced my experience of the world. As a Fellow of the Rockefeller Foundation during these six months, my program was as follows:

Part 1 - The first four months in the United Nations (January to April)

Two months - in the Department of Reference and Documentation

(a) Reference work (in broad form).

(b) Inspection of special departments.

(c) A few days in the U.N. Archaeological and Map Collection Department.

One month spent in departmental libraries

(a) Two more weeks at the Security Council Library.

(b) Two weeks in the Economic department library.

Part 2 - Fifth month (May)

After gaining full practical experience of the Library of the United Nations, I inspected the following libraries and educational institutions:

New York City and Vicinity

(a) Columbia University and all its departmental libraries, including the Teachers College Library.

(b) New York Public Library—Central and Branch Libraries.

(c) Libraries of special subjects, such as Engineering Societies' Libraries, Medical Libraries and other similar libraries.

(d) Montclair, New Jersey Public Library and its branches.

(e) The Yale University Library.

Boston, Moss

(a) Harvard University Library, Widener, Harvard College of Business Administration and other libraries.

(b) Boston Public Library.

(c) Massachusetts Institute of Technology Library.

Washington DC

(a) Library of Congress

(b) Army Medical Library.

(c) Pan American Union Library.

Nonvilla, Tennessee (Up to a week)

(a) At the invitation of the officials of the Tennessee Valley, I went to see the rural library service work of that state.

Part 3 - Sixth month (June)

U.S. National Archaeology, Washington D.C.

*****

To utilise my evening hours, I attended evening classes to learn French at the United Nations, Lake Success.

It is my personal experience that wherever I went, I was well received everywhere. When I went to Tennessee, I was afraid that my complexion might hurt anyone, but nothing special incidence happened.

You would probably know that just as we have *Harijans* at our place, similarly there are negligent people here who do not get that much status in the society. For them the seating area is different, the schools are different and everything else is different. I will write about this in more detail sometime.

I travelled in coach class instead of first class to save a few dollars. Also sat in first class which is called Pullman here, but not always. Instead of staying in hotels, I stayed in 'Young Men's Christian Associations' (YMCA). Here a room is available for one and a half to two dollars, which is cheaper than the hotel. Apart from this, the atmosphere of Y.M.C.A. is also better than a hotel.

The US-tourism lead ended on 30th June. After that I was getting a very good appointment in the United Nations Library. But mother's health was deteriorating day by day. She, as you know, was in a semi-neurotic state due to my absence. I was also keen to return home. Apart from this, if I stayed there for more days, 'Rockefeller Foundation' could have forfeited the fare for my return to India. In such a case, I would have to pay for the ship out of my pocket. So I decided to come back to India. As a result, on

14th July I left New York by a steamer belonging to American Lines. I had this firm determination in my mind that I would come again to pursue Ph.D. God helped me and I came to do Ph.D. and got success in doctorate.

For the first time, I had written the full story of my journey from New York to London, which I had sent to my revered father when I came to London. It's all in one file. I had been even writing about the journey from London to Bombay in the letters from time to time. Europe tourism details have also been written.

You might have liked this account of my first foreign trip. When I started telling you this story two years ago, I hoped to tell it in more detail; but the study and research work was so stressful that I could not devote much time towards this. This is just a sketch of the story. Whenever I get time, I will sit down and write with details and try to make it fit so that more people can enjoy it.

I also think that I should write a chapter each on the social, political, economic and educational life of America and also express my opinion on that life and environment. I will write this when I get time.

******

927 Sylvan Avenue
NR class
Michigan (U.S.A.)
Date July 21, 1950

Dear Prem,

In the first twelve letters, I wrote to you the details of my departure from India and stay in America. Hope you found it interesting. In the thirteenth, fourteenth and fifteenth letters, I am sending you a copy of the pages of my diary which I had written during my travels in the ship 'Vendam' and 'SS Canton'.

13

New York to London

Our ship Vendam, whose picture I am sending you, left at exactly 3 o'clock in the afternoon. It was scheduled at 12 o'clock; but due to the workers' strike, it was delayed for so long. As seen from its drawings, the ship is 15,500 tons in weight, 575 feet in length and 65 feet in width. It has about 350 workmen and passengers are around 1000. It has two classes. One is first class and the other is passenger class. There are separate rooms for first class passengers while three passengers are sharing one room for passenger class. The rooms are fitted with electric fans, carpets, and hand-washing basins. The rooms are very clean and the beds are cleaned daily. The dining room is huge. Separate table and chair are there for each passenger. There are also four passengers at a table. There is a waiter at every two tables. There are nice tablecloths on the tables. There are bouquets of fresh flowers, which are changed daily. Food is very good. I told the main chef here yesterday that I do not eat meat. For me now people serve only vegetables. The food is fresh and pure. The fruits are also fresh and good. Milk is also very tasty. You can eat bread & butter as much as you want.

Many chairs are lying on the top floor of the ship, which is called the deck. They also have mattresses on them. Passengers spend most of their travel time on these chairs only. From here the view of the endless ocean looks great. Wherever you look, water and only water is visible there. When the ship moves through the water, big waves of water are formed. This sight is a treat to watch.

There is also a library on the ship. The playroom, restroom and sitting room are separated. There is also a barber and a liquor store. The rooms are decorated like a king's palace.

There are residents of about 20 countries on this ship, out of which 3 people are Indians. There is also a *Sardarji*, who came to America 30 years ago and got married here and became an American. He has got his hair done. Yesterday, I happened to talk to him for about an hour on various topics. Everyday variety of movies are shown here.

July 15, 1950

This morning I woke up at 6 am. After dealing with daily chores, I went to sleep again. Breakfast is served here at 8 o'clock. For breakfast, I took *Chakotra* (Grapefruit) juice, fruits and coffee. Actually not just breakfast, but a good amount of food. After breakfast, I went to sleep again and got up at 11 o'clock. I sat in the sun on the deck for an hour and started watching the waves of the sea. Had lunch at 12 o'clock. Vegetables were specially served to me in the meal. After the meal, I ate two apples and drank a glass of milk. A movie was shown at 3 o'clock.

It is 5 pm now. I will sit on the deck for a while and then have dinner at 6 o'clock. After the meal, I will sleep on the deck. The weather here is quite cold now. Cannot go out without a coat. Seasonal wind is very cool and fragrant. The stars look great, as if the buds of the white vails have been scattered.

July 16, 1950

Today is Sunday. I woke up at 7 o'clock in the morning. Finished morning chores in half an hour and went to breakfast at 8 o'clock. The stomach was full of breakfast.

After that I came to the library and talked for some time with an Indian brother. Then there were separate prayers of Catholics and Protestants. I attended both. When the prayers were over, an old lady came towards me and said are you an Indian? I said yes! She asked if I knew *Mehar Baba*? I replied that I have definitely heard the name but did not get a chance to meet him. The woman told me that she was an American woman and a devotee of *Mehar Baba*. She also told me that she was planning to invite *Mehar Baba* to America next year.

Thus it is 11 o'clock. Then I thought of getting a haircut. I went to the barber shop and he made my favourite hair in about 20 minutes. His fee was 35 cents and the tip was 10 cents. Tip is not a custom at our place. Tips are given everywhere here. Washed my head after haircut. Just then it was 12 o'clock and the food bell rang.

Somebody called, 'Now have some food.' If you had eaten in an English hotel, you would have understood this description very well. There is a heap of forks and knives on the table. Three types of knives and three types of forks.

The boy who serves three types of spoons and changes the saucers about seven times. When one thing ends, he brings another thing. It takes 1 hour to eat like this. This poor man has to bring some vegetables for me. The person serving appears to be less than 20 years old. The food is served in large quantity that it becomes difficult to manage it. That is why I rely more on fruits, fruit juices, milk, butter, and ice cream. After having dinner today, I asked my other companions how many people in the world get enough food. Those poor people didn't have any idea. They came from America where much of the food is destroyed in the ocean. I said that 75 percent of the people in this world do not get proper food two times a day, especially the exploited inhabitants of Asia.

Now just listen to the condition of the people sitting at my desk. This is a complete family. There is a husband and wife. Going to their country Germany after 30 years. They have three boys and one girl. The boys are young and the girl is 6 years old. He is a very nice man. Today he was drinking wine. Told me too when I said I don't even know its taste. Offered me a cigarette too. These people are surprised to see me. Looking at my food, he says "How do you survive." I said as I have been living with you for the last three days. Similarly, about 26 years of life have been spent.

Well, these people do not know the importance of these things. They are completely materialistic. Their culture is completely different from ours. After dinner, I came upstairs to the deck. Today was a great day. I began to sunbathe on a comfortable chair. There was a program to show a cinema at 3 o'clock. The cinema ended at 5 pm.

Then I thought that I should fix my further plan. I had to clear my doubts as to when I was to leave from Southampton (London). However, before I started, I came to know on the phone that on 28th July I had to go to Bombay from Southampton port by Canton ship. But I wanted to confirm. Hence I sent a counter-radiogram to the P&O Company in London. I am waiting for a response. If I want to leave Southampton on the 28th, I will go straight to Paris from here. Staying there on the 25th, I will see the nearby country Switzerland. I will come to London on the 26th. Staying in London on 26th, 27th and 28th, I will leave for Bombay from Canton on 28th.

It is 9 o'clock at night now. I am sitting in the lounge of the ship. Almost all the passengers are playing cards. Some are talking. These are mostly rich people. Some people are also drinking beer and wine.

There will be a concert in the dining room after half an hour, i.e. singers will play guitar and English type instruments. I'll also go and listen.

I had expected that I would have sea sickness, but it was not even felt that I was travelling on a ship. The ship is moving at a great speed of 15 miles per hour. You will be surprised to hear that the speed of ships is 15 to 20 miles per hour. Now I am sitting on the comfy chair outside the room. The moon is hanging like a sickle in the sky. Although it is now 9 pm; But still a little redness is visible. There are waves in the sea and the ship is crossing them and heading towards London.

July 17, 1950

It was 10 minutes before 8 o'clock in the morning, when I woke up. I finished morning chores quickly and came for breakfast. I was not hungry today. Even then I took two glasses of orange juice, a glass of milk and ate bread along with coffee. The waiter had also brought two apples for me. I ate them too. I had slept so much but I don't know why it was not full of sleep even then. I slept late last night, maybe that's why I slept till late in the morning and still did not get full sleep.

When it was 20 minutes to 12 o'clock, the room cleaner came and woke me up to tell me that it was time to eat. I sat rubbing my eyes and came up dressed in clothes. There were only 8 minutes left at 12 o'clock. So I went to the deck for fresh air. Just then the bell rang. The food today also was as interesting and substantial as usual. He had brought special vegetables for me. I cut two apples and ate. My stomach was full.

Today was as good as yesterday. The sun was very strong. I sat on my comfy chair. Then when the sun started getting very hot, I started watching the waves of the sea and like this it was 3 o'clock. Today again at 3 o'clock a cinema was shown, which was very humorous. The name of the picture was 'The Good Humour Man'. This cinema ended at 4 pm. Then I sat on my chair. An old woman was sitting there. She had come from Holland. I started talking to her. There was talk of Indonesia as well. You know that Indonesia was a colony to Holland as India used to be of England. It was important that she pointed it out as Indonesia's fault. About Panditji she said that "I don't like him."

You will remember that Panditji had called a meeting about Indonesia in India. Many such discussions kept happening. At this moment the bell rang for the food and our conversation ended here. I went to eat food in the same manner and returned after eating fruits.

The day before yesterday, I had made the assistant engineer here as my friend. Today I met him again. I asked about how the ship is working. Tomorrow he is given noon time to explore. I will meet him tomorrow and he will show me all the machinery of the ship. This will be my first time seeing the ship's machinery. The cinema will be shown again today evening. Then I'll go to sleep.

बकिंघम महल

Buckingham Palace

July 18, 1950

Today I woke up at 7 am. Had breakfast at 8 o'clock after finishing with other daily chores. After breakfast, I fell asleep and rested till 12 o'clock. Fasted this afternoon because I wanted to give some rest to the digestion process. As a result, I felt very hungry in the evening. And ate food full of heart. Food was also of my interest. There was also fried potatoes and spinach *saag*. Fruits and ice cream were available regularly.

I went to see the ship's machinery at 1 o'clock this afternoon. It was very heavy. This ship runs on steam. Steam is made from oil. Electricity is also generated in the ship itself, ice is also made, which is used to keep food cool and does not allow it to rot. The ship's engineer told me about almost all the necessary things.

By this time we have come to a distance of about 1300 miles from New York. Southampton is 3000 miles from New York. We will cross this distance by the coming Sunday. Our ship travels about 328 miles in 24 hours.

It is colder here today than yesterday. Today the sun was not so strong. Even then we were still in our respective chairs. Today I met an old English couple, who came and sat beside me on a chair. This old man had gone to India in 1897. The year when there was an earthquake and famine in Bengal was there. I exposed the British. To my surprise, he himself appreciated my point and told it right. He himself told me that when there was a famine in Calcutta in 1897, the British government was sending food grains out of India. Then we talked to the extent that Indians taught bribery to the British. He also admitted that he too used to take bribes. Nowadays these people live in Bristol, East Indies. Their eldest son is married, so these people are staying in London and are engrossed in enjoying life.

At this time, the day is almost hidden. The darkness of night is slowly spreading its black sheet. The blue sea has also turned black. The ship is moving at a slow speed. Today we also saw big black water animals. These animals are called sharks. Apart from this, snowy mountains were also visible. Tonight the game will be shown till 9 o'clock and a very melodious instrument was played during the meal.

July 19, 1950

I woke up today at 7 am. There is an Englishman in my room who is used to getting up early in the morning. Seeing him, I find out the time and then take the route of breakfast.

After having breakfast as usual, I went to sleep and woke up at 10 am. Got up and went to the deck for fresh air. In the meantime, the elderly *Sardarji*, who has now become an American, peeped from above and came down and started reciting the sweet memories of his childhood. He told in a very interesting way about the difficulties he faced while coming to America how he started earning. But I didn't like why he became American. Even then their existence or non-existence do not make any impact on India.

After the meal, I came upstairs and started counting the waves of the sea. It turned to 3 o'clock while doing so. Then I went to see the movie. The name of this movie was - "Adventures of Captain Good". This movie was full of action. Then I came up and read the newspaper.

So far I have not mentioned that newspapers are also published on the ship. Every day an eight-page newspaper comes out of the ship's newspaper office, which is distributed to almost all passengers. The ship's oversight office has a wireless, radio and tele printer. There are also reports of India's ongoing treaty talks with Russia and America. It is apparent from this that even though we are in the lap of the ocean, we are not separate from the civilised world.

The evening meal was also fun. Fruits and ice cream were also available. The sea is still very serious. No fuss of any kind. Half the journey has been completed and half is still left.

I got up at about the usual time today. That's how the day passed. But so far no response has been received from London to the telegram I sent to know whether my itinerary has been confirmed to depart from Southampton (London) on the 28th. I am waiting for tomorrow. Otherwise, I will get off the ship at Southampton itself and will set the stage for France and Switzerland. Nothing new happened today. Same food, same conversations with people, movies, happy faces and ocean waves.

Friday
July 21, 1950

I woke up today at 7 am, then went to sleep after breakfast. I slept little today. Then I went to the deck at 10 o'clock and kept talking to the people. Had lunch, watched a movie at 3 o'clock.

After dinner I came to the library and discussed various subjects with the passengers.

Today I started reading by taking a book from the library. The book is "Charles Dickens - 1812 to 1870".This is the biography of England's Una Pope-Hennessy. Charles Dickens was a great novelist. I had also read Dickens during my college days. I like this author very much. He has painted poignant pictures of the oppressed class in his novels.

Saturday
July 22, 1950

Today after breakfast, I came to the library and the whole day was spent reading books there. Today there was very little traffic on the deck due to winter. Yes, I definitely went for a morning tour. I have finished most of yesterday's book, I will read it completely by tomorrow.

Today, new waves of enthusiasm are rising in my mind. The biggest reason for this is that we are approaching London. We hope to reach Southampton at 5 a.m. on Monday, then reach London at 11 a.m. by taking the 9 o'clock train. All the passengers of the ship are filling various forms to reach their designated destination. Those who are going to London need not to fill it, because India is still in the Commonwealth. That's why I don't even need a visa. Yes, going to France and Switzerland a Visa will be required which I got in Washington itself. Now I am sitting in the library. The ship is moving at the same speed, parting the waves of the sea. I wanted to take a picture of these scenes but couldn't take it yet. If it's sunny tomorrow, I'll definitely take a photo.

Sunday
July 23, 1950

Today all the passengers were excited, happy and enthusiasm was visible on their faces. The day was also temperate. The destination of the passengers was drawing near. Around 2 o'clock in the day, after walking for the whole nine days, some land was visible. A few more ships appeared. The world's largest and best ship 'Queen Mary' was also seen. It was going from London to New York. The speed of this ship is more than other ships. It travels about 30 miles an hour and reaches New York from London in 5 days. Rest of the ships take 8 or 9 days. I haven't taken a single picture since I got on the ship. I took a lot of pictures today. I will bring them as memories.

Farewell dinner was given to all the passengers in the evening. On demand will be served from 10 o'clock in the night. The luggage of the passengers getting down at Southampton has been arranged. Tomorrow at 5am we will reach Southampton. A large boat will come to pick us up in the sea and it will drop us to the train.

July 24, 1950

Today we reached Southampton at around 7 am. Then I came to London by car. This evening I will decide when I will come to India. As soon as I know, I will send a letter to you.

London
Evening July 24, 1950

I have sent the details of the journey from New York to Southampton in the afternoon. It has also been decided in the evening today that I will leave Southampton at 5 pm by a ship called Canton on 28th and reach Bombay on 13th August. Now I am waiting for the train to Paris. I will also go from Paris to Switzerland and then come back to London.

I didn't like London. Compared to the huge cities of America, all the cities of the world seem to be villages. The rail, house, food and drink here are all old fashioned. There are restrictions on some food items. But there is so much food in America that things have to be destroyed in the sea. I will also write you a letter from Paris.

Have you decided to come to Bombay? In my opinion, if any of you want to come then come. Here I will meet Rajjo and Chote (relatives). Mother does not need to come to Bombay because money is tight. Further you decide. I will write the rest when I reach Paris. Jai hind to mother!

London
July 28, 1950

Today was my last day in London. I was staying in "Indian YMCA.". It is run under the authority of an Indian Dr *Malaiparaman*. In another sense it is a hotel for Indian students. It's "YMCA." is divided into two buildings. The building in which I am staying is smaller than the first one. About 15 students live in it. There are four other Indian students in the room where I am staying. There is no provision for bathing in it. The urinal pot for urinating and the wash basin for washing hands and mouth are also very aged. The arrangement of hot water is also not like America. In other words, everything here is just for the sake of being here. For food and snacks, we had to go to another building. However, this house was the cheapest and I had to spend only two nights.

I went to the Regal Hotel at 9 in the morning. Two years ago a friend had left shirts here, I had to get them. After this I came to the room, arranged the luggage and wrote three letters. Vacated the room by keeping the luggage outside and deposited the keys in the office. I got 10 shillings from the office which I had deposited earlier as security. I then met Mr. Palmer, a prominent worker of the British Library-Association. Then came to the P & O office by taxi and confirmed about the ship. After dealing with the necessary things and paying the custom duty etc, I left by the ship at exactly 5 o'clock in the evening. Also took some pictures on this occasion. The name of this ship is Canton and P&O is the company that owns it.

The ship weighs about 16,033 tons and carries about 2,500 passengers. It runs from Southampton to Hong Kong. Most of the travellers are from India, Sri Lanka and Hong Kong. The management is lenient in this ship, the food is also not tasty. Those who serve are more into appeasing the British. Butter is not to be seen, because there is ration on it. I hope from tomorrow, there should be some different food and drink arrangements for vegetarians.

It is now 10 o'clock in the night. I was very tired from today's clutter. I will sleep now. Currently I am sitting in the restroom. Some people enjoy playing cards. Some are gossiping. There is also a library in this room. I am thinking of reading some books. But now I will be able to read tomorrow only. Okay, Jai hind.

14

London to Bombay

From London to India
(Ocean)
July 29, 1950

This was the first day of my departure from England to India. Nowadays I have breakfast at 9 o'clock in the morning. Lunch is at 1 o'clock and in the evening I eat dinner at around 8 o'clock. Good nutritious food is not available like the earlier ship.

The whole day was spent in the library reading books and talking to co-passengers. I saw a movie in the evening. It was an American film, whose name was - 'Dancing in the Dark'. I had seen it before also.

It is now 11 o'clock at night. I am sitting in the loungeroom on the upper floor. The white rays of the moon are scattered in the sea. The weather is very pleasant.

July 30, 1950

Today's weather was much better than yesterday. As we are proceeding further, the climate is also changing. Today we saw the border of Portugal. It seems that a lot of shipping happens on this sea. The sea is still calm, but there are signs that the ocean will become stormy after the Suez Canal.

Nowadays, I get up at around 8 o'clock. The steward keeps "bed-tea" at 8 o'clock in the morning and also brings oranges along with it. The first thing to do when you get out of bed is to drink tea. After that I shave and wash my hands and face and go to the toilet. I have breakfast around 9 o'clock. After breakfast, I read books in the sun. When the sun becomes unbearable, I go to the lounge room.

The nature of the passengers in this ship is different. There are many Englishmen in this, who are either going to Colombo, Hong Kong or Singapore. They are people with business instincts. You will know that we have stopped trades with England. The trade between India and England is negligible. Many people are also angry, so I try to explain to them. Some of the passengers even accept, while some remain rigid. They are of the view that India is not doing so well. They claim that India has been given independence by the British at will. Perhaps they forget our national movement and the unprecedented political consciousness of the Indian people.

Sometimes I even participate in games. But I am not very interested in them.

This ship has a separate room for children. There are many toys in this room and there is also a nurse. Mothers leave their children in this room after breakfast in the morning. This nurse takes care of children. The room is closed by the main door made of bars. Today I stood in front of the door of this room and watched the children playing for a long time. Among them are some toddlers too. I loved to see them playing. I got almost Indian style food on this ship. I eat to full stomach and Mango chutney is also available. But here milk and curd are not available. Because there is a ration in England on milk. So far the ship is going well.

July 31, 1950

As our ship kept moving towards India, the heat became more and more. Evening weather becomes very pleasant. My old friend who once studied together at St. Stephen's College, Delhi brought records of English songs with him. He made me listen to many songs on the upper floor. The moon also rose in the sky, as if it too wanted to hear the songs. The air was soft smelling. This program continued till 11 o'clock in the night.

The sky was covered with twilight and mist since morning. The speed of the ship also slowed down and started giving whistles again and again so that no other ship could come in the same path. The mist kept its empire till noon. At last the sky became clear and the sun came out, as if a beautiful blonde had peeped through a veil. Gibraltar also came on the way, but due to the fog nothing was visible.

A lot of debates took place today. I got people on my side with my arguments. An English passenger, with whom there was half an argument yesterday, started saying that your eyes have strange looks, which got stuck in the heart. In English such eyes are called 'piercing eyes'. He also started saying that you win half the game because of your eyes. I can't say to what extent this is okay; but many people have the same opinion about my eyes. There is a *Sardarji* also in my room. His name is S. D. Singh. He is an engineer and a very warm-hearted man.

August 1, 1950

It was hot all day today; but the weather turned good at night. Around 6 o'clock the moon also came out and started shining. I sat on a chair on one side of the ship and watched the moon rise. Cold rays scattered on the sea. I wish! I would have been a good poet. I wanted to take a couple of pictures. Finally came to my cabin and took pictures with the camera. Maybe the pictures turn out to be good. Because the ship was shaking, I suspect nothing may turn out well. I was about to go to bed at 12 o'clock. Some colleagues asked me, "Why don't I drink alcohol?" On this subject, I gave them a few examples and explained the reasons for not drinking and they appeared somewhat impressed.

It was the first time I took a bath since I stepped on this ship. There are two types of water for bathing here. Sea water is salty and the second is sweet water. After mixing cold and hot water in the tub, lie down in it for some time and then, take a bath with sweet water to clean the salty water.

Our ship is reaching Port Said on the 5th. Hope to stay there for a few hours. If the weather is fine, I'll take some pictures too. The weather is hot. I don't even like it. The journey is quite long. Slowly all the days will pass and the destination will come nearer. There is a hope in every moment.

August 2, 1950

Today's day also passed like reading and writing, talking and watching the waves of the sea. Today we saw a big island called "Malta". It is in the possession of the British. It was bombed by Germany during the war. Seen large fishes also in the sea.

After dinner, I listened to the records of English songs with my friend. Then I went to sleep. The weather was still hot today. But somehow the day passed.

August 3, 1950

Nothing special happened today. Day was hot. It was boring and drowning in sadness. I kept reading books all day. I slept after lunch. Woke up only after drinking tea in the evening and then sat down and started reading again. After dinner I saw a movie which was full of laughter and belonged to an American Film Company. Spent some time in the open air at deck and then fell asleep around 12 o'clock

August 4, 1950

Even today no special incident happened about which I should write.

The same food and drink, conversation, reading a book and the buoyant waves of the ocean kept my mind engrossed.

Port Said (Egypt)
5 August 1950

The ship stopped today after travelling for a full 6 days. Our ship arrived at Port Said (Egypt) at 5 am. Not exactly on the shore, but a way was made to reach the shore. I got up at five o'clock in the morning and at 6 o'clock I had finished bathing. The cabin mates woke up quite late. They thought that after breakfast at 8 a.m. we would go for a city tour. We were ready to leave the room at 7 o'clock.

I came up to the deck with my camera and passport and started asking permission to enter the city. Cameras were not allowed on Port Said, because it is a region of the Suez Canal where photographs are not allowed. Because the Suez Canal is a large canal and very mysterious from the point of view of fighting, no one is allowed to take photographs.

Port Said is the meeting point of Western and Eastern Civilization, or rather, the first introduction of Eastern Civilization comes from here.

On the point as the ship enters the port, there is a statue of Ferdinand de Lesseps, the engineer who built the Suez Canal and named after Fouad I, the father of the present king of Egypt. There are also office buildings on the same side of the Suez Canal. Many ships were seen on this port. There were ships from almost all the countries of the world. One ship was from India too.

Port Said has a population of 120,000. From May to October Climate is cold at night and hot during the day. From November to April there is little cold and sometimes rain, but the night is cold throughout the year.

History of Suez Canal

The Suez Canal was inaugurated in 1869. This canal was taken on lease by the British for 99 years which will end in 1968. The length of the canal is 100 miles. Its width is 200 feet from Port Said to Ismailia. This canal enters Lake Timsah at Ismailia. From this place, another lake is about 20 miles long, which joins Bitter Lake at De Vorsorge and after that it becomes somewhat narrow and enters "Little Bitter Lake" at Cabaret. Upon leaving "Little Bitter Lake'" the ship enters Port Tyjic which offers a spectacular view.

I went to visit the city with two of my friends. What city, it was a small town. There were different types of shops, which can be compared with the shops of Hapur (Uttar Pradesh - India). The sellers of many things on the way clung to us like honeybees. Getting rid of them was a problem.

Leather goods are said to be quite cheap here. But people here are not honest. An old seller came after us. And when we bought two leather goods, he left the chase. The friend bought a lot of things.

I haven't bought the watch yet. I needed a watch. The buckle of my father's watch broke a year ago. But the clock was still running. I went to an Indian watch shop and bought a watch. The shop was also big, the men were also good. I was not really at a loss. The clock turned out well. An English traveller sold many watches because of Custom duty. He asked for 7 dollars for an American watch. He gave it to me for 4 dollars. Looks good and is running fine so far. But not bad for four dollars i.e. 20 rupees.

After walking around the town, we got back on the ship at 11 o'clock. It was very hot here in the room. The weather remained the same for the whole day. But the night was cold. Sitting upstairs in the company of some friends, I kept watching the Suez Canal. Then around 12 o'clock the moon also rose. It was a beautiful sight. I don't feel anything great compared to this scene. The soft moonlight coming from the moon like nectar being spread from a nectar bowl. I don't know why these atomic bombs and hydrogen people do not see such scenes. Why do they prefer human genocide? Why not use nuclear power for human development?

Every moment was pulling me towards home. Heart was so elated. At 12 o'clock I came to the cabin and slept.

ईफल टॉवर—पेरिस

Eiffel Tower

To Aden
August 10, 1950

I am writing a letter today after 5th August. In these five days, the heat caused a lot of trouble. The high heat between Port Said and Aden continued to disturb. And nothing special happened.

After several days of heat, we reached Aden yesterday morning. The ship stayed here for about 6 hours.

At about 8 o'clock we got down from the ship, sat in a boat and crossed the sea and reached Aden by taxi. Aden looks like a small town and is only 3 miles. Ship to shore costed 10 *anna* and the return also took the same amount of money. The total fare for travelling in the taxi was 8 rupees.

Aden is said to be the first diamond of the Crown of Queen Victoria. It was annexed to the British Empire in 1839 and remained under India until 1 April 1931. After this it was made a colony. It is the most important oil and fuel supplying station in the East. The length and breadth of this colony is 75 miles and the population including Little Aden is 80,000. English, Arab, Somalis, Indians and Jews live here. The climate is pleasant in November and March.

The scene of Aden was like reaching to a Muslim homestead. This town is surrounded by two big mountains. The colour of the mountains is ochre *(an earthy pigment containing ferric oxide, typically with clay, varying from light yellow to brown or red).* I took many photos here. Although the ship had to depart at 12 o'clock. I returned back at 9 o'clock only.

The sea was a bit calm as we moved ahead from Aden. But the situation in the Arabian Sea got a little worse. Thick walls of storm water shook the ship. I was feeling sick, so I didn't even get up. Didn't even have breakfast. Around 1 o'clock I came upstairs to the deck and started playing deck tennis to amuse myself. In the evening there was a fancy dress show and dance. Shipmen call it the Gala Evening.

The dining room was furnished. There were strange hats on every table. There was a Turkish hat on my desk. I wore it. I brought cabbage leaves from the ship's kitchen. I also made my cap and hung a garland of leaves on my head. I wanted that black colour to be found from somewhere and it should be rubbed on the body and then cleaned with soap; But could not get it even after trying. Yes, the colour of the clothes was definitely found, which was more long lasting. So the idea of using it was dropped. That's why I wore a dress of leaves without any colours. But my thoughts could not be met due to lack of some important things. I took off the garlands and came upstairs dressed in clothes. There I saw other passengers in strange clothes. Two of my Indian friends had become bride and groom. Similarly, dressed themselves as per their wish and imagination and who stood best and strange, got rewarded too.

Now English dance is going on. Indians, British, and travellers from other countries are engrossed in the dance. It was only a delay of asking the girl with whom you want to dance with. Almost everyone is drinking alcohol. They are immersed in the pleasures of momentary life by swinging in fun. There are colours spread everywhere, and I am writing this diary.

Seeing these scenes, if someone wants to compare India and English civilization, then he will get many good ideas from here and the difference will also become clear. It is very difficult to say exactly which civilization is good; but each civilization has its own merits. I do not like English civilization, the structure and conduct of its society at all, but I like their qualities. The civilization of India was created according to its climate and its many needs, the civilization of the British was also built in the same way. English civilization has not been able to find its footing in India, but some of its descendants have been adopted by the people. Our society today is being ruined by caste-based, untouchability. We can learn this quality of English civilization to remove these diseases from our civilization. It is now 12 o'clock in the night. It's time to sleep. I'll write the rest later.

August 12, 1950

Tomorrow we are reaching Bombay. A dream that I had seen four years ago has come true. Or rather, I am returning today after completing it. It is very difficult to say what I have learned in these three years, and what I could implement. Meanwhile, I got the opportunity to meet people of all ideologies.

Some of my companions used to drink alcohol, ate meat, indulged in indulgences i.e. they were complete hedonists. But I am glad that I could not fall into his thoughts and they could not drag me down the wrong path. When I did not go on their path, some called me bad, some insulted and some got angry. But like a hard rock, I remained steadfast on the path of truth.

Today is the last night on the Canton ship. I also hope that I will still go abroad for higher studies. The ship is going well. After leaving Aden, the sea was stormy. Many passengers were victims of vomiting. I was nauseated after waking up only one day. Nothing happened after that. The weather had changed a lot. It was quite cold in the evening. Today the weather is not too cold. I hope the weather will not be too hot when I reach Bombay. I don't have cotton clothes. It will take too long to prepare the new ones.

Our ship is reaching the port of Bombay tomorrow morning. By about 11 o'clock the passengers would get down from the ship one by one. Then we have to get free from Customs. Then only we will be able to meet our relatives.

15

Return from my first overseas travel

On August 15, 1950, when the ship named SS Canton, on which I travelled from London, came close to the Bombay port, it was 6 o'clock in the morning. There was fog everywhere. I remember very well that I was standing on the deck and looking at the port without blinking my eyes. The turrets of the Taj Mahal Hotel were visible. The "Gateway of India" scene was a reminder that my motherland has arrived. The passengers of the ship seemed very excited and were handing over their belongings to the ship's officers and keeping a few light items and necessary papers in their hands lined up on the deck. Their eyes were looking for their friends and relatives standing on the port building visible from far, who had gathered there to welcome them. The speed of the ship had slowed down. And the navigators were turning the ship inside the port. This process must have lasted about an hour when I saw that the ship had entered the harbour. Two stairs were installed for the passengers to get down. One stair was for first class passengers, the other for excursion class passengers. There was also a difference in the decoration of the stairs. I was standing on the deck with my camera. My thirsty eyes yearned to get a glimpse of my parents. It was difficult to find them because of the crowd. There was also a difficulty that the greeters were waving umbrellas, handkerchiefs and watches in their hands and trying to find their acquaintances. After a long time, I saw my mother peeping out of a window of the custom office and then my father was also visible. *Lala Jankinath* was also standing where my parents were, at whose place my parents were staying. I took many pictures with the camera in which their pictures were also captured. Passengers were going to disembark and only those people stayed in the ship whose relatives had obtained permission to board the ship from the port-officers. After a while, they also got down and reached the huge building of the Custom office. Seeing the complicated proceedings of the tax authorities, I thought about how well the westerners make arrangements so that no traveller has to suffer in vain.

My turn did not come even after standing in the queue for an hour, while the acquaintances or the people who were tempted were doing their work by violating the limits of the "queue" system.

Sometimes I would request people to be in the "queue" but my voice went mostly unheard. After an hour and a half my turn came and the tax officer looked at my form with great attention and turned it upside down and said that Rs 45 of the duty to be paid. So I gave a note of 100 rupees and after examining the note, he returned the remaining amount. Then I came to the big hall where my belongings were kept which were arranged according to the name of each person. I could see the chaos here too because some gentleman came to the tax office and didn't know what magic he did. His goods were released without any screening. Another young man had climbed up from Aden and was our cabin mate. Seemed naïve and not very educated and appeared to be a businessman. The tax officer did not take much time to get into the depths of his feelings.

I was surprised to see that he had fifty *tolas* of gold and other things which he wanted to save from the custom duty. Everything was taken from him. But after a while a middle-aged gentleman came out dressed in muddy clothes and shook hands with two or three officers in front of me. As soon as the handshake was done everything was fine. That is, shaking hands meant giving a bribe.

This gentleman took his belongings and I don't know how much money the tax officials took away as a gift. When I cried for justice, they were a little embarrassed at my humble request. The tax officer told me that we are sorry that you had to wait. I said, "I am a student and have filled out the custom items in the form." Not only this, I also offered him my bunch of keys and said that you can open the goods and check. My words gave him another strength and he got confidence in me and got my stuff released. After loading all my belongings on the porters, I came outside the customs house and got the goods kept in the car which had come to pick me up. In no time my car (in which I was seated) along with the other car in which *Lala Jankidas* was sitting came under the building of Gadodia Bank on Kalbadevi Road on which we were staying on the third floor running parallel on the broad streets of Bombay.

After about two years, there was an auspicious opportunity to meet the parents. For an hour the conversation about the changes in the family went on. Then we had food. This was my first-time seeing Bombay. I expressed my desire to see the famous buildings of Bombay to *Lala Jankidas*. Luckily that day was August 15th. The whole city was decorated with lights, flags, paintings, and festoons. There was enthusiasm in the public. The desire to see the mesmerising nature of *Juhu* grew stronger. On boarding the bus, we saw the city's wide markets, tall buildings, mill chimneys, buses, trams and cars and then reached a place where there were thousands of dirty huts, in which people lived a very hellish life. Later on asking about it, I came to know that there are lakhs of such people in this city who do not even have such filthy, cramped and damp huts and they sleep on the footpaths only. Cook here, sleep here. Little babies are born on these tracks and die here. At this moment, the thought of the splendour of Europe-America and a prosperous civilization flew out of my mind, which I had returned to after seeing and living among them and I felt as if it was a dream. Oh! These Indians, oppressed by extreme poverty, neglect of humanity, exploitation. I was engrossed in these thoughts that the bus took us to *Juhu*. We got down with full excitement and saw that the deep ocean was pounding in front of us.

The water seemed to have descended a little that day. Up to far away only sand was visible instead of water. We got down in the sand and came to the place where *Gandhiji's* statue was installed. It was established here after his death. The importance of this place is also believed to be that *Gandhiji* came to rest here after being released from jail in 1943. I took a picture with the camera. A green coconut seller was sitting near that idol. When *Lala Jankidas* requested me to drink green coconut water, I could not say no. I drank this for the first time and it was very tasty. Then I also ate coconut kernels. Just walked to the Palm Beach Hotel. There I had to meet a relative who is also a successful actor. When traced, it was told that he lives in another part of this hotel. To my surprise, I saw that this part was made of huts. My relative had gone to Bikaner at that time for a movie, so had to return disappointed. If he would have been there, we would definitely have gone to some studio. After a while we came back by bus. Interacted with the people who I met after having food. Then I slept. On the second day, after breakfast, I set out to see the Archaeological Museum of Bombay, Zoo, Hanging Garden and other attractive and scenic places. Museums and zoos, however, weren't that much of an attraction to me because I had seen the world's great museums and zoos in New York. Near the Gateway of India, it suddenly came to mind that the British had made all this to leave a historical memory of their civilization, art and valour. Near it was the huge building of the Taj Mahal Hotel, where Indians and dogs were not allowed to enter a few years ago. What a shame it was that we Indians could not go there even after spending our money, whereas it was created by Indian labour and money.

After Gateway of India we went to see Hanging Garden. This is a very beautiful place. This garden is built on a water tank whose water is distributed to the whole city of Bombay. On both sides of its beautiful streets, there were gleaming mansions of the eminent people of the city of Bombay. Proceeding further, we reached a beautiful flower-filled park. There the green carpet of grass looked very nice. Also the fencing was cut artistically and it would look like lions, camels and elephants were standing. No doubt it was a classic example of horticulture. The cool-mild-fragrance breeze and sometimes a little cloud-splash would make the mind elated. I also took many pictures. Then we came back.

We came home, had lunch and met a cloth merchant who had just returned from Japan. He mentioned that if we send ready-made clothes like sleeping suits etc. from India to America, it will be of great benefit because labour is very cheap in India and very expensive in America. I said that on one hand the Government of India will allow such trade with difficulty, on the other hand the custom duty is also considerably high and thus the same high prices will be incurred. At the same time, the American government does not want their standard of living to decline. There are more than enough things to eat and drink. They are either given to a friendly nation or destroyed at sea. The talk was going on that he said let's go, let me take you to see the temple of Hanuman ji. Apart from the Hanuman temple, we also took a tour of some scenic places. After returning home, I had dinner and slept at around 11 o'clock. Thus after spending two happy and memorable days in Bombay, I came to Delhi with my parents.

Many relatives and well-wishers were present at Delhi station and it was an immense pleasure to meet all of them. A week was spent in meetings like this. The world-famous Dr *S. Ranganathan*, who is called the father of library science in India, was in America at that time while I was away. They wanted me to reach Delhi at the earliest and take charge of the Department of Reference of Delhi University which was being commenced recently. He only had stopped me from going to Italy and Switzerland for the purpose of my early return to India and postponed my seat in the plane which I had reserved for going to those countries.

Simultaneously, after he asked Mr. Lall, the Passage Reserve Officer of the Rockefeller Foundation, I got my seat in Holland American Lines' ship S.S. Vendam. As soon as I came to Delhi, I met Prof. *S. Dasgupta* and he immediately got me an appointment letter from the Vice-Chancellor. I started the work with great zeal and put a plan in front of him which was given great acceptance and I was asked to go ahead. Within a few days, this department became popular among research students and library science students.

Meanwhile, Dr Horace I. Paulman, who was the cultural attaché of the American Embassy in India in those days, had come. I was trained under him in the "Library of Congress" in Washington DC. When I met he asked what I was doing? I said that I am setting up a "Reference Department" in the University of Delhi as a reference librarian. He said with a serious note that the American Embassy is planning to open libraries in many places in India, and you will be very suitable for the purpose. Initially, we will give you a monthly salary of seven hundred fifty rupees.

I did not have much experience of the ups and downs of life, as a result, I hastily accepted his words and resigned in Delhi University. Dr *Ranganathan, S. Dasgupta* and other friends did not like my decision. I started to work at the US Embassy; but from the very beginning, the atmosphere there started pricking me. I was influenced by national sentiments from childhood and took an active part in the national movement from my student life. I didn't get a chance to do work organically there. There, only orders had to be followed. Everything in that American library was American – the books, the magazines, the furniture was American. That is, it was a one-sided world and was forced to look only on one side. The thoughts with which I had pursued higher education were suffocating. As a result, I started feeling sad. It was decided in my mind that after staying for a few days, I should save money so that I can go abroad for higher education again.

When 7 or 8 thousand rupees were collected, I met Mr. *Nandalal Mehta*. He was already known to me. He asked what you are doing. I told everything. And I expressed the desire that I have compiled the published literature on Gandhiji in 12 languages in the form of a book. Fortunately, he knew *Mr. Mavlankar*, who was then the head of the "Gandhi Memorial Fund". Mr. *Kaka Kalelkar* who had been appointed as the Director of "Gandhi Memorial - Museum" was staying with Shri *Mavlankar*. He introduced me to him. Seeing my work on "Gandhi literature", he was stunned. He said that the "Gandhi Memorial - Museum" set up in Bombay is being brought to Delhi and that is why the Government of India has given four rooms in "Kota House Annexe". It will be great if you support us for the cause. When he came to know that I was offering my services for the US Embassy, it struck him. He inspired me to work for my country and said that even if my country gives less money, even then it should also be accepted. You are young now. The uplifting of the country will come on the shoulders of youth like you. If you are not able to make sacrifices for the uplifting of your country, then how will the freedom achieved by the sacrifices of lakhs of crores of Indians flourish? These words of Dada *Mavlankar* had a magical effect on me and I decided to resign the very next day.

Exactly a month later, I resigned from the US Embassy and took over the task of running the Gandhi Memorial Museum. During this month, the goods which came from the Bombay Museum loaded in the goods train. My companion Mr. Pandya and I brought them to the "Kota House Annexe" after loading them in handcarts. As the work progressed, two assistants were added and every effort was made to catalogue and classify the books, manuscripts and photographs we had with us. When I was engaged in this work, the feeling of going abroad was getting stronger day by day. I was in correspondence with the University of Michigan. They had accepted that I could make Gandhi's bibliography as the subject of the thesis for my PhD. This was only one part of pursuing the PhD, I had to also pass five examinations on different aspects of library science and tests in French and German languages. I have always been prepared to face the greatest difficulties to fulfil my desires. Therefore, no matter what difficulties may come, I decided that I will definitely do a PhD. This time I did not have to go through the hassle of getting a passport. I got the period of my passport extended for five years by paying a fee of Rs.10. The tricks for getting a visa from the US embassy were also known to me. I have given the necessary documents this time also. But this time I did not have to give the impression of my ten fingers, because it was already with them.

16

Second overseas travel

This time due to the fellowship from the University of Michigan, it was convenient to get the visa. This time I already had saved some money with me and some more had to be arranged. Like before, this time there was no difficulty in getting the passage. In order to experience all kinds of ships, I reserved a seat in a cargo ship. The ship was named SS Cape Town and it departed from a port in Calcutta at 9:30 pm on 10 July 1952. The remarkable thing about my life at this time was that I was married now and was about to become a father. In those days my wife was staying with her parents in Calcutta. Leaving my wife in this condition (when she was about to become a mother), and who was standing near the ship and had come to bid me adieu, I boarded the ship, then strange feelings started coming in my mind. But the determination of higher education gave me support and strength and gradually the past memories disappeared and a twinge settled in my mind.

The ship slowly sailed through the bottomless sapphire waters of the Bay of Bengal and proceeded towards Ceylon. The Bay of Bengal has always been famous for its storms. There was a huge storm that day too. The SS Cape Town, whose weight did not exceed 10,000 tons, began to dance to the thuds of the waves. This time I had made complete arrangements to avoid 'sea sickness'. My friend in Delhi presented me with a few pills which proved to be very beneficial to avoid 'sea sickness'. These pills are named Dramamine and they are yellow in colour.

Next day we reached *Visakhapatnam*. When the ship stood in the bay, Mr. *Mookerjee* and I (who were travelling along in the ship) went to see the city which was very beautiful. There we drank fine coffee and wrote some letters. In the evening we reached Madras and went there to visit the city and we ate dinner at YMCA. After travelling for two days we reached

Colombo where we stayed for three days. This was my first time to see Colombo. There were big buildings near the port. There were English-style markets. Branches of big banks were there and English civilization was reflected there in the same way as it is in cities like Calcutta, Bombay and Delhi. Mr. Mukherjee and I went to see Colombo University and also saw the race grounds near the university. Also visited a well-known ancient Buddhist temple in which the images of Lord Buddha were inscribed in different postures. Then also saw the Legislative Assembly of Sri Lanka. This place was on the beach and was situated in a huge ancient building. We did not have the admit card so we could not enter. It can be said that it was by no more impressive than the Parliament building in New Delhi. We had lunch in a Ceylonian restaurant. The food though was of Indian style; but the chilies were more. As a result, I could not eat much and had to be content with only a few fruits. We also saw an American movie. The movie-hall was a temporary hall which upon enquiring was found to have been built for the war-soldiers. Seeing the movie, we returned to the ship at 9 o'clock in the night. After gossiping for some time, we fell asleep.

The next day our ship had to depart in the afternoon. After breakfast in the morning, we went out roaming. Bought picture postcards from the post office and sent greetings to friends and relatives. Then we went to the city for a few hours and also bought some things. We returned at 1 o'clock and stood in the ship and watched the ships coming and going in the port. After a while our ship left for Aden. The ship had only stayed for a few hours in Aden so we could not get off. However I was not eager to get embark because I've seen it before. After a week's travel from Aden we reached Port Said. Stayed there for a day, then headed straight to Boston. This journey was very rough and hard too. When the ship reached the port of Boston, huge buildings were visible. When the ship stopped, a tax officer and a doctor verified our papers. The doctor inspected my medical report and also saw my chest X-ray and after finding me healthy, allowed me to get off the ship. After this the custom officer opened both my leather chests and saw them himself. But not seeing any item worthy of custom, he wrote OK with chalk. The same thing happened with Mr. Mookerjee too. Then we started getting down from the ship, then shook hands with the officers of the ship and bid farewell. Some servants, who used to serve our food or clean the room, met us. It didn't take me long to understand what it meant. So according to our reverence, we got down after giving them the award. There was a taxi waiting for us. I had to go to Ann Arbour which was about 900 miles from Boston. I did not want to carry the entire luggage with me because of the burden. So I booked a briefcase for Ann Arbour by rail, which was not needed on the journey. After booking our luggage, we came to YMCA. Boston and stayed there with a room. My hair had grown a lot, so I got them cut by a barber and as a reward I had to pay one dollar and 25 cents as tip, which in Indian currency was equivalent to about 6.5 rupees. After hair dressing I came to YMCA and took bath after six weeks, changed clothes, went to the cafeteria with Mr. Mookerjee and had a full meal. It was almost one o'clock by this time. After resting for a while, we went to see Harvard University.

My friend Mookerjee had to meet a relative who had just got married. I also had to meet Dr Bhatnagar and Sridhar, who had been professors at the University of Delhi. We did not know their addresses, so we saw the list of students at this year's university and found out the addresses. First we went to Dr Mookerjee's relative's house. Coincidentally, he had organised a banquet to celebrate the wedding on the same day. So when we reached, we could not avoid his request. After so many days, the invitation of Indian style food was indeed a matter of joy. After finishing the meal, Dr Mookerjee took us for a tour in his car. Of course, how beautiful the first day in America was. First seen some historical places of Boston, where the first battle between America and England took place in 1779. This is a very wide space. There is also a statue of a soldier standing here who fired the first bullet and that too became immortal by being a victim of British bullets. Some sentences were also carved on a rock in which the battle of British and American was described. A small river was also there and a bridge of ancient times was also built on it. Small boats were also being rowed. Different types of flowers were blooming in flower beds on both the banks of the river. This scene was very beautiful. Returning also saw the house of the great saint Emerson and also saw the museum established in his name. The place is at a great height and the entire city of Boston was visible from the car. There were green hills on both sides of the road. Dr Mookerjee dropped us off at YMCA where we rested for the night. I took a bus to New York in the morning and came to New York in the afternoon.

In New York, I stayed with my friend *Sardar Surjit Singh*, who studied with me at the University of Michigan in 1948-49, and now works in the library there. *Sardarji* served me Indian food. On the second day I reached the Indian Embassy branch where I met one of my old friend and neighbour Mr. *Prakashchandra Jain*. I had lunch with them too. Then came to Columbia University, where in the evening I went to the International House. The International Building of New York occupies a very large place among the International Student Buildings of America. Where students from all countries of the world come and settle down and take education in Colombia

University. International spirit is awakened by meeting them, having conversations and also participating in discussion.

The next day I went to the UN where I had worked for the first eight months. There were many friends there too. Among them were Mr. *Sikan,* Mr. Patel, Mr. Roberts and many officials of the UN Library. After many years it was a great pleasure to meet them and I ate lunch with him.

My friend Surjit Singh also introduced the new employees of UN who joined after 1950. Had dinner with them in the evening and after dinner, started walking towards the International Building. Had a conversation with some friends there and slept. On the third day I met Mr. *Prakash-chandra Jain* again in the office of the Indian Councillor. I needed a typewriter. Mr. Jain sold his typewriter for 55 dollars. He took us to his house and then we started towards our residence. That day was Saturday. The number of students was more in the drawing room than on other days. Got acquainted with many new Indian and foreign students. Then moved towards *Sardarji*'s house at 10:30 pm. The next morning, along with Sardarji, loaded my luggage in the taxi and headed towards the "Greyhound" bus station. There Sardarji made me sit in the bus and went to UN and I started towards Ann Arbour. After travelling for two days, I reached Ann Arbour. There I connected with a friend from Mathura who had come to America with me in the same ship in 1948. He showed great respect and made arrangements to stay with another friend who had plenty of space. In the meantime I had reorganised my old living space where I lived in 1948 and 49. The owner of the house is a lady. Her name is Mrs. Palmer. I always call her mother. Surely she is a great mother. The days I lived in America I never felt that I lived in a foreigner's house on rent. She supported me in every sorrow and happiness and treated me like a son. Her sons and daughters-in-law were also kind to me. I lived in this house till 20 September 1954. I will always be grateful to these people and their memory will always be etched in my heart. Surely such mothers are blessed.

17

Preparation for PhD in Ann Arbour

As soon as I arrived in Ann Arbour, I went to meet Professor Gelsness, Chairman of the Department of Library Science, and my mentor, Dr Kilgar. However, the admission had already been done; but after consulting him, a plan for PhD was to be made. After consulting him, I made a program and decided to do research accordingly. Here, like the admission of 1948, this year also a long form had to be filled. Medical examination was also done. When there is a medical examination, every boy and girl is asked to take off all their clothes and keep them in bags provided by them. The medical examination of boys and girls is held at different places. Then for each part of the body, there is a separate specialist who sits in the line and examines it by instruments. A chest X-ray is also taken. Inspection of stool and urine is also done. This medical exam takes about two and a half hours, and in the meantime every student has to remain completely naked. In this way after about 3 hours I completed the medical examination. Then the picture had to be taken to get the 'identity card' made and the pre-filled form was taken to the 'Admission Hall' and handed over to the concerned departments. Also paid the first study-time fee and returned to Michigan Union with the receipt where I had lunch. Then I read the newspapers of that day in the 'International Centre' and listened to the news from the radio and met friends. I stayed there till evening and came back home after having an evening meal. The studies started next day.

The pattern of doctorate in American universities is different as compared to English and Indian universities. A student is only allowed for PhD when he passes the supplementary examinations. French and German examinations also have to be passed, then only permission is given to write a thesis. After a year of hard work, I passed the 'complementary exams' and also cleared the French and German language exams. Now writing the thesis was easy for me, as I had been researching my topic for many years. I will always remember that I used to work from morning till 2 o'clock in the night. I finished my thesis in *April 1954*. This thesis was so big that it took a month to get it typed and I got three copies prepared. One copy to the University of Michigan and two copies to the Department of Library Science so that members of the doctoral committee can read the thesis conveniently.

Now I had to pass another tough exam! That too an oral examination of about two hours. The date was also fixed and I did some preparation as well. At around 3 o'clock the members of the committee started examining me and it continued till 5 o'clock in the evening. Then the committee president went to another room to consult the members and in about 15 minutes,

Dr Kilgore started congratulating me with a smile, my happiness knew no bounds. The dream I had 15 years ago was being fulfilled today. I bid farewell to all the members and to Dr Kilgore. My friends were also happy for my success in PhD.

I sent two telegrams, one to my parents and the other to my wife and father-in-law and wrote two memorable words "P-H.D Vijay" (Won PhD) After sending the telegrams, I came to Michigan Union. My mouth was dry. Ideas seemed to flow. Hunger disappeared due to happiness. I went straight to the International Centre where some friends were waiting. As soon as I entered through the door of the drawing room, *Shri Raghuveer Prasad*, who was not only my neighbour but a good friend, rushed towards me and started congratulating me. It was a very auspicious and great day for me. After a while some more friends came and started congratulating me. I sat among them for about an hour and then left to have food fearing that the cafeteria might get closed. After that we went to see the cinema. After returning from there, I slept happily.

The convocation ceremony was to be held at the University of Michigan on *15th June 1954*. The convocation there takes place in a large stadium where 95,000 people can sit at once. This time the University of Michigan was gifting a hood to students who passed out for PhD and D.Sc. My friend *Mr. Raghuveer Prasad Lat* had fully intended to take colour pictures; but as soon as we reached near the stadium, it started raining the way it had never happened in America before. After about an hour and a half the rain stopped. The hope was that it would not rain again, but when the convocation ceremony started, it started raining again. As a result, the President of the University and the honourable guest had come to participate in the convocation ceremony and left after finishing their work within some time.

It was the shortest convocation in the history of the University of Michigan. The students took their degrees and hoods and went to their respective places of residence. I also went to the 'Michigan Union' with some of my friends and had dinner with friends there. Mr. Lat, who could not take my picture there, advised me that this occasion does not always come, so the photo must be taken in this 'academic-dress'. He took me to a photographer's studio and there I took several poses, from which I chose one and I got the enlargement done.

After the convocation, I stayed in Ann Arbour for three more months as there was practical training which I consider necessary from the point of view of experience. Along with this, I used to get three hundred dollars per month for expenditure.

At the end of the training, I had to leave Ann Arbour and packed my luggage and left for New York by bus in the evening. After coming here, I stayed for five days and started making plans for my return.

18

Return from New York to India

On the 17th of September 1954, I woke up early in the morning, and went to the room on the fifth floor of the huge building - The International House, New York, where I had been staying for a week. When I returned from the bathroom, I met two young students from Bihar who were a little nervous about the hustle and bustle of New York. Washing hands with soap after defecation after putting Janeu on the ear. (One of the most famous and sacred rituals is that of wearing a Janeu. It is a sacred white thread which is worn by the brahmin boys on reaching the age of twelve and called 'Upanayana Sanskar'). The word 'Upanayana' means the sacred vision to see things. Seeing his Yagyopaveet, I remembered my own Yagyopaveet, which was missed while taking off clothes while leaving India. During the conversation, I smiled and asked where did you come from? In answer he said nervously that we both landed in New York last night by plane and were going to Colorado to receive Mining training. I asked eagerly do you have another Janeu? One of the brothers looked at me in amazement and said do you really need a Yagyopaveet? I said - "yes". He ran and brought the sacred Janeu from his room and, along with chanting, I wore the Yagyopaveet (The ***Yagyopaveet*** Sanskar is performed to channelize this development. The initiation is through Gayatri Mantra). Thanking him, I returned to my room and got my stuff done.

It was now 7 o'clock. I had to reach the place by 8 o'clock from where the MS United States ship was about to depart. I brought my luggage down from the elevator and returned the key after paying the room rent and took the security money back. After that I called a taxi which arrived in two minutes. I sat in it and came to the banks of the Hudson River and entered the port by showing my passport and sailing permit at the gate. I had already sailed my heavy baggage from Ann Arbour itself, which was kept safe in the basement of this ship. I was carrying only a suitcase and a handbag. Which was brought to my cabin by a porter.

This ship (M.S. United States) is America's largest, comfortable and luxurious ship. It is the fastest and built with the latest technology. It is 960 feet long and 101 feet 6 inches wide. It is 53,300 tons heavy. It first left New York on 3 July 1952 and returned from Europe on 10 July 1952. It reaches London from New York in about 5 days while other ships take 9 or 10 days. I reached the deck at 9 o'clock. My luggage was picked up at the deck door and delivered to the ship by a machine. I entered and showed my ticket and sailing permit and boarded the ship. First I reached my cabin where my luggage was kept. Putting luggage etc. on my berth

I came to the common room where my friend was sitting with his parents and sister. They had come to see-off their daughter who was going to study English literature at the University of London on the fellowship of the USA. We sat there talking till the ship did not sail. When the ship departed, the dinner bell rang and we went to the dining room. Including me there were four passengers at our dinner table.

Two of them were going for a trip to Europe. The third girl was my friend's sister. These people were naturally non-vegetarian; but being a vegetarian, I ate a lot of fruits, fruit juices and boiled vegetables. We were also given a copy of the "Passengers List" in which my name was also printed. This ship also had a good cinema. There was a barber shop, a well-equipped children's playroom, dancing hall, hospital, post office, market, library, smoking room, bank, type room, cathedral and printing press. This ship was like a big city. Each room was air conditioned and had a phone. There used to be indoor and outdoor games also every evening. There was a bathing pool too. This ship was like the palace of a King. Its living rooms were made of luxurious wood. There were carpets everywhere. These five days passed as if I had reached a magic city. Five days later the ship reached Southampton. From there I reached London by train and stayed at the "Indian Student Hostel" where I had already made arrangements to stay. Participated in the first three-day meeting of the "Association of Scientific Libraries and Information Bureau" (ASLIB) in London and saw the main landmarks of London.

On 28 September 1954 at 4 pm, I left for Bombay by boarding "SS Liberia" on the P & O Line. This was the first voyage of this ship, as it was commissioned last week only. It is the largest and heaviest ship of the P & O line. Its weight is 29,600 tons. Its length is 718 feet 9 inches and width are 90 feet 6 inches. This ship has two classes - First Class and Tourist

Class. There were 674 passengers in the first class and 733 passengers in the tourist class including me. It had 711 staff employees. Altogether there were 2,115 people on the ship. The dining room in this ship was air-conditioned. Other facilities were as on the first ship. The next day there were four people including me at the dinner table. Two were Sri Lankans and two were Indians. One of them was a doctor, the other was a student at the University of Cambridge, who had just returned after completing a doctorate in economics.

The waiter who served the food was very lazy and always used to forget to bring a saucer of vegetables for me. Somehow, 14 days were spent and after crossing the Red Sea we came to Port Said, which has a population of 120,000. This Port Said is located at the northern entrance of the Suez Canal. It is a port town, so all kinds of shops are found nearby. Leather goods are available here in bulk and at cheaper prices. Our ship stayed here for about 10 hours. I went to the market with some of my friends and bought a leather bag, wallet etc. My companions also bought some things and after about four hours of roaming we were back on the ship.

The ship had left at 10 o'clock in the night. After a while it entered the Suez Canal, whose account I have written in the description of the first journey.

After 4 days our ship arrived at Aden and stayed there for about 8 hours. We also went to visit the city and bought something. Vital among them was the clock. After Aden, we reached Bombay after travelling for 5 days, this time it was around 6 o'clock. From afar, the lights of 'Gate of India' and "Taj Mahal Hotel" were visible. In few moments the ship entered the port and we began to prepare to descend. My mother's health was bad this time. So she and father could not come; but younger brother *Shraddhanand* (my cousin) and *Pt. Ajay Singh* (my father-in-law) had come to meet me. *Shraddhanand* had obtained a permit to board the ship. When I met him, my happiness knew no bounds.

After getting though the customs we came out of the building and sat in the car of Lala Ram Niwas and reached his residence which is situated on Marine Drive. Umesh Sharma, who is a close relative of mine and is well known as a good actor, took me home where I stayed for the night. The next day we took a tour of Bombay and also visited a studio. After staying there for one more day, I came to Delhi by evening train with Shraddhanand and Shri Ajay Singh. Father, friends, my wife, son and acquaintances had come to meet me at the station. We were meeting after 3 years. How pleasant was this union after this period of separation! When I reached home, Mother was sitting and waiting. I touched her feet and felt blessed. A wave of emotional and physical happiness had no bounds.

This was the last day of my second overseas travel and return to India.